TWAYNE'S WORLD AUTHORS SERIES

A Survey of the World's Literature

Sylvia E. Bowman, Indiana University

GENERAL EDITOR

FRANCE

Maxwell A. Smith, Guerry Professor of French, Emeritus
The University of Chattanooga
Former Visiting Professor in Modern Languages
The Florida State University

EDITOR

Montaigne

TWAS 317

Montaigne

By MARCEL TETEL

Duke University

Twayne Publishers, Inc.: : New York

Library of Congress Cataloging in Publication Data

Tetel, Marcel.
    Montaigne.

    (Twayne's world authors series, TWAS 317. France)
    1. Montaigne, Michel Eyquem de, 1533–1592—Criticism and inter-
pretation. I. Title.
PQ1643.T4   844'.3   74-2250
ISBN 0-8057-2623-3

Contents

About the Author

Marcel Tetel has been teaching French and Italian at Duke University since 1960. His interests lie in Franco-Italian literary relationships during the Renaissance. He has written several studies on Rabelais: *Étude sur le comique de Rabelais* (1964): *Rabelais* (Twayne, 1967); and *Rabelais et l'Italie* (1969). His most recent publication is *Themes, Language and Structure in Marguerite de Navarre's Heptameron* (1973). This present study on Montaigne will lead to a comprehensive work on Montaigne and Italy.

Marcel Tetel has been the recipient of an American Council of Learned Societies Grant-in-Aid (1963), a Fulbright Grant to Italy (1966–67), a Guggenheim Fellowship (1970), and an American Philosophical Society Grant (1973). He is currently Chairman of the Department of Romance Languages at Duke University.

Preface

Writing about Montaigne offers two critical alternatives more distinct than in most authors: to crystallize what his mind thinks or to delineate how his mind thinks; both focus on content. In the latter approach, not only is the thought process an important subject in itself, but its impact on the topics it deals with bears directly on the configuration an idea will take. Because little controversy exists on the ways Montaigne's mind works—he circles an argument from several vantage points in time and space—this approach can produce assured results. On the other hand, to offer a synthesis of Montaigne's thoughts presents difficulties due precisely to his manner of thinking. If constants do surface from his intellectual undulations, it is quite conceivable that a number of arguments on a given topic do not take their rightful place in the discussion, and it is only this omission that allows a synthesis. Furthermore, what role does irony play? Its presence would certainly undermine any crystallization of opinions. Can Montaigne's views on religion, politics, ethics, existential conditions (for example) be neatly packaged?

The Renaissance mind explores much more than it takes definite stands on issues for any length of time. And a broad synthesis under the aegis of naturalism, relativism, or wisdom (the famous *sagesse*) offers a simplified solution. Ambiguity and paradox already give some insight into the critical complexity, although they do not satisfy those who would like a more palpable answer. These difficulties of interpretation explain the publication of at least seven excellent books on Montaigne just in the last twelve months, and attest to the enduring and self-renewable quality of the *Essays*.

In this book we do not claim to have broached every topic contained in the *Essays*, nor to have brought to bear every essay on a given argument. The vast variety of subject matters and the large number of essays (one hundred and seven of them) preclude any such comprehensive treatment in a relatively short space. However, we have attempted to include all important topics and some that have not traditionally attracted much attention but have begun to come to the fore recently, such as ambiguity and paradox, communication, nescience, the inadequacy of language and structure; in all cases we have put our own stamp on any discussion. In addition to the better-known and longer essays, we have also tried to bring to light some lesser-known and shorter essays, such as "Of Thumbs" and "Of Riding Post," pieces sometimes shunned by critics, but which deserve more critical attention because of their denseness and microcosmic functioning in relation to a larger whole. Finally, we have not dissociated form from content, since in the *Essays* form is content; syntax, structure, Montaigne's smile, metaphors also shape the meaning.

This book deals essentially with the *Essays*; the *Travel Journal* to Italy, Montaigne's other major work, will not receive much attention here except as it bears sometimes on an argument or an essay. This choice is made because the *Essays* is by far the outstanding work and contains more than enough material for critical appraisal. Yet this reason does not quite excuse the exclusion of the *Travel Journal*. On the surface, this diary—much of which, dictated to a servant, was never intended for publication and has the appearance of a documentary travelogue—relates much more of what Montaigne does than of what he sees when he arrives in a city, but he always sees people rather than things. When Montaigne takes over the composition of the journal, he writes in Italian: *Assaggiamo di parlar un poco questa altra lingua* ("Let us try to speak a little that other tongue"). Significantly enough, the first word he writes is "try"; the Italian *saggi* means essays. The journal is deceptively matter-of-fact at first glance and awaits further critical attention—but not within the context and the aim of this study.

The reader will note that the chapters of this book become progressively longer. This progression registers the very close interrelationship among topics—how one of Montaigne's concerns can hardly be separated from another—and the intimacy of form and content. Anyone who starts writing about one subject in Montaigne finds that others insist on appending themselves automatically; this phenomenon is the delight and the difficulty of reading the *Essays*.

MARCEL TETEL

Durham, North Carolina

Chronology

1533   February 28: Michel Eyquem is born in the family chateau of Montaigne to Pierre Eyquem and Antoinette de Louppes, both belonging to wealthy merchant families.
Calvin takes up the banner of the Reformation.

1534– M. receives his first formal education at home from a German
1539   tutor who teaches him to speak Latin, but no French.

1539– M. studies at the Collège de Guyenne of Bordeaux, whose bookish
1546   methodology he will later deplore. This period witnesses the beginning of the Inquisition in Italy (1542) and the opening of the Council of Trent (1546). In 1541 Calvin translates into French his *Institutio Christianae Religionis*, first written in 1536, and Copernicus publishes *De Revolutionibus* (1543).

1544   Birth of Françoise de la Chassaigne, M.'s future wife.

1547– M. studies, first, philosophy at the University of Bordeaux, and
1559   then law at Toulouse.
In 1549 appears the *Défense et illustration de la langue française* by Du Bellay, and in 1550 the first poetry by Ronsard.
François I dies in 1547 and is succeeded by Henri II.

1554   Pierre Eyquem, elected mayor of Bordeaux, relinquishes to his son Michel his duties as Councillor at the Cour des Aides of Périgueux, which will be incorporated into the Parliament of Bordeaux three years later.

1557– M. is councillor in the Parliament of Bordeaux. Henri II dies in
1570   1559 and so does his successor François II in 1560. Charles IX accedes to the throne. Beginning in 1562, religious conflicts more and more take on the appearance of civil wars, especially in the regions around Bordeaux.

1559– M.'s friendship with Etienne de La Boétie, fellow councillor in
1563   the Bordeaux Parliament and an indirect creative force behind the *Essays* after his death. The same year that La Boétie dies, 1563, the Council of Trent ends.

1565   M. marries Françoise de la Chassaigne, daughter of a fellow councillor. Six daughters will be born from the marriage, only one of whom will survive, Léonore.

1568   Pierre Eyquem dies, and Michel, being the eldest of four sons, inherits the domain of Montaigne.

1569   M. publishes the translation of Raymond de Sebond's *Theologia*

Naturalis, a task he had undertaken upon the wish of his father and La Boétie.

1570 Taking advantage of a respite offered by the peace of Saint-Germain, M. retires from the Parliament and leaves his post to Florimond de Raemond, who is to become a highly militant head of the Catholic side.
After a sojourn in Paris to oversee the publication of La Boétie's works, M. retires to his domain.

1570– M. begins to write his *Essays*.
1571

1571 M. is ordained into the Order of St. Michael and receives from Charles IX the title of Gentleman of the King's Chamber.

1572 Soon tired and bored with being involved in new constructions on his lands, M. spends his time in the famous tower-library of his chateau. August 24: Massacre of St. Bartholomew's Day.

1574 May 11: M. addresses the Parliament of Bordeaux in the King's name, and urges that the city be placed in the state of defense against the Protestants.
Charles IX dies; Henri III comes to power.

1578 M. suffers first attack of kidney stones, followed by sojourns at spas in the Pyrenees.

1576 Formation of the Holy League pitting the Catholics, headed by the Guise family, against the Protestants.

1580 March 1: First edition of the *Essays*, composed only of the first two books, and published in Bordeaux. June 22: M. begins a seventeen-month journey to Italy via Switzerland and Germany, ostensibly to visit spas. A diary kept during this voyage will be discovered almost two centuries later and published in 1774. At the outset of this trip, M. detours through Paris to offer in homage to Henri III a copy of his recently published *Essays*.

1581 While at the spa of Lucca, M. learns of his nomination as mayor of Bordeaux, which the King hastens to approve, and M. returns to France to assume his duties.

1581– M. is mayor of Bordeaux for two terms, the second term more
1585 difficult than the first because of renewed civil and religious war.

1582 Second edition of the first two books of the *Essays*, in Bordeaux.

1585 June: The plague breaks out in Bordeaux. M. absent from the city, decides not to return to preside at the election for his successor; instead, he retires to his chateau and will write essays.

1587 Third edition of the first two books of the *Essays*, in Paris.

1588 New edition of the *Essays*, containing for the first time all three books and six hundred additions to the first two books.
In Paris M. meets Mlle Marie de Gournay, who becomes his adopted and spiritual daughter. He attends the Estates-General of Blois.

May 12: Day of the Barricades; Henri III flees Paris, fallen to the League, and orders the killing of Henri de Guise.
The Spanish Armada.

1589   Against Paris in revolt, Henri III appeals to his cousin Henri de Navarre and both lay siege to the capital. When the League sees all is lost, they have Henri III assassinated. Henri de Navarre succeeds him as Henri IV. Death of Catherine de Medicis.

1590   Marriage of M.'s daughter, Léonore. First Italian translation of the *Essays*, most of the essays of the first two books only, by Girolamo Naselli.

1592   September 13: Death of M. while listening to mass in his room. Buried in Bordeaux in the church of the Feuillants.

1595   New posthumous edition of the *Essays*, edited by Mlle de Gournay, containing the additions made by M. between 1588 and 1592. The text of this edition was transcribed by M.'s wife and Pierre de Brach from an annotated 1588 edition in M.'s handwriting; this annotated volume is referred to as the Bordeaux Copy.

1601   Death of M.'s mother at the age of ninety.

1613   First English translation of the *Essays* by John Florio.

1616   Death of M.'s daughter Léonore; she had given birth to a daughter in 1591.

1627   Death of M.'s wife, Françoise de la Chassaigne.

1633–   First Italian translation of the entire *Essays* by Marco Ginammi.
1634

1655   Approximate date of the famous *Entretien* (interview) by M. de Saci with Pascal on Epictetus and Montaigne, published in the eighteenth century. This interview was in essence a test by M. de Saci before admitting Pascal among the solitaries of the Jansenist monastery at Port-Royal.

CHAPTER 1

Essaying

W HEN Montaigne began writing his *Essays,* sometime around 1572, he was the first in French Literature to choose this genre, and he has not been surpassed by any one since. In England, of course, we have Charles Lamb's famous *Essays of Elia.* In American literature, only Ralph Waldo Emerson, himself an ardent admirer of Montaigne, has gained equal fame as an essayist, and the modern Spanish author Ortega y Gasset also stands out as an adept of the essay. But in French literature no other first-rate author dominates in this genre; the modern Alain, for example, certainly does not belong to the very best of this century, and the eighteenth-century Diderot, who shares much with Montaigne, is an outstanding figure, but not primarily remembered for his essays. This uniqueness of Montaigne endures.

Was Montaigne aware of the new path he was cutting? Or did he simply stumble into it by following the lead of his own temperament? Since eight years elapsed between the time his first pieces were written and the publication of the first two books of his *Essays* (1580), it is quite conceivable that upon initiating his writing career, Montaigne was conscious rather of setting down a commentary on current notions and ancient adages than of writing in a genre; he was groping for both form and content. At some point during these eight years, we do not know when, he decided on the title "essays" for these writings. We do know, however, that the term "essay" preoccupied him, for it occurs at frequent intervals, both as a substantive and as a verb, throughout his work. What it indicates is a growing consciousness of a developing genre—and the difficulty of the creative and thinking process.[1]

I *The Meaning of the Essay*

When the genre at last emerges from the probing and the experimenting, it fuses form and content in perfect fashion. The word "essay" derives from the Latin *exagium*, a weighing. Indeed, the *Essays* are a succession of weighing, balancings of opposites along the whole gamut of philosophical and existential problems from life to death. In them Montaigne offers us a kind of compendium on how to face the human condition. By definition, an essay is a trial, that is, an attempt and an experience; each is thus meant to be a self-testing or tryout (but also a mere sampling or taste) in an unterminating apprenticeship. An essay is an investigation of a subject, but not its possession; it probes a reality with a succession of hesitant contacts. It is also a thinking process, an effort to "think oneself" and thus to create oneself. In Montaigne's case the reality is fragmented into his mind, his body or self, and his literary work. Thus the *Essays* are consubstantial to Montaigne; they form one substance with him; he is the *Essays* and they are he. And in the end he can rightfully proclaim that they constitute "a record of the essays (experiences) of my life" (III: 13, 826).[2] Yet by their very nature they are inconclusive rather than final. Their paradoxical existence does not, however, lead to nihilism; on the contrary, their ultimate value lies in the testing of judgment for self-knowledge, the essence of the *Essays*.

The function of a Montaigne essay, thus, is to discourse critically on a problem and to declare the current state of a subject matter or question. It follows that the answer matters less than the road traveled to reach it, the peregrinations of the thought process. An essay is worth more than a resolution because the passage, the traveling of the mind, surpasses taking a position, since any position is inherently tentative and bound to be supplanted by others. Yet Montaigne does take stands; he is forced to do so many times, and, as a matter of fact, his *Essays* surprise us by adding up to an encyclopedia of knowledge. He holds forth on religion, ethics, all forms of human interactions, love-marriage, government and politics, education; he considers himself a moralist, a psychologist, an autobiographer, a sociologist, and an historian. Philosophical isms attract him and result directly from his observations and experiences; stoicism, epicurism, skepticism, and naturalism occupy places of varying importance in the *Essays*. All these endeavors and vocations are cast in the context of time by which he is haunted; the concept of duration both brings out and conquers mutability. And the act of writing and how to write and the consciousness of it leads to a progressive self-knowledge, to a form of permanence, and reinforces the consubstantiality basic to the *Essays*.

However, the search for knowledge and for the self uncovers

the lies and errors of human opinion. Hence, the ultimate function of the essay is to analyze the illusions and impostures of any affirmed posture. Montaigne's own position as a writer comes into question; he often considered himself a plagiarist, and others made the same accusation, but even though his essays sometimes resemble marquetry or mosaic, the components form the writer and the writer forms them. He essays himself against them, and they are transformed into essays and multifarious images. In fact, the *Essays* owe their very formal and ideological originality to the composite nature which gives a particular organic unity to the work. Literature is the transformation of form and content into another whole; and these transformations matter foremost.

II   *The Reading Public*

For whom was/is the *Essays* written? In a short foreword "To the Reader," Montaigne answers the question. But does he answer it quite as candidly as he makes show of doing?

This book was written in good faith, reader. It warns you from the outset that in it I have set myself no goal but a domestic and private one. I have had no thought of serving either you or my own glory. My powers are inadequate for such a purpose. I have dedicated it to the private convenience of relatives and friends, so that when they have lost me (as soon they must), they may recover here some features of my habits and temperament, and by this means keep the knowledge they have had of me more complete and alive. (p. 2)

It can be safely assumed that Montaigne never meant this work to be a private diary not for the public eye since he himself oversaw its publication at various stages. The *Essays* was of course addressed to an educated public. Whether Montaigne expected no glory with posterity from his toil remains a debatable question. Again it can be safely assumed that he would not have taken pen in hand if he had not felt threatened by death and the thought of complete oblivion with future generations. Genuine modesty is not and cannot be one of the virtues of a writer.[3]

From the very outset, "To the Reader" raises the more important question of Montaigne's sincerity. When does Montaigne's smile lurk in the background and when does it not? Its presence can no longer be denied, as will be amply demonstrated. This smile has a marked impact on the meaning and nature of Montaigne's thought. Its existence in the *Essays*, however, attests to another form of essaying—trying out the reader's credibility and playing with it.

When placed in context, later statements negating glory stress the mutability of time and above all of language. In one of his last essays Montaigne again repeats that he does not have posterity in mind: "I write my book for few men and for few years" (III: 9, 751). By the latter phrase he hints that his book will soon be forgotten because it is not composed in Latin. Surely he could not have meant this; half a century before, Calvin had translated his *Institutio Christianae Religionis* into French in order to assure it of more readers. Stendhal also wrote for the happy few, so he claimed, but at least he was less ingenuous, since he forecast that he would be famous a century after his death. Montaigne proclaims instead the brittleness and insufficiency of the language he presently uses:

In view of the continual variation that has prevailed in our language up to now, who can hope that its present form will be in use fifty years from now? It slips out of our hands every day, and has halfway changed since I have been alive. We say that at this moment it is perfected. Every century says as much of its own. I have no mind to think that of it as long as it flees and changes form as it does. It is for the good and useful writings to nail it to themselves, and its credit will go as go the fortunes of our state. (p. 751)

The last sentence lets the cat out of the bag. Montaigne hopes indeed that his *Essays* will belong to the category of writings that nail language to themselves, that forge and essay language in spite of its deluding and mutable nature.

III   *Achieving Instable Stability*

Yet the process of essaying, probing, is most evidently acute in the realm of content, where the mutability of thought and variety of human nature dominate. The same process, however, in the domain of structural form is more fixed and buttresses the shifting content. In this vein, the order in which the essays were published attests a conscious design. The first essay in the first book, for example, "By Diverse Means We Arrive at the Same End," was composed at some time in the 1578–80 period, shortly before the publication of that book; the next twenty essays date from the 1572–

74 period, while, with very few exceptions, the rest of the essays were composed during a broader six-year span that also begins in 1572. But Montaigne chooses to open his book with a specific essay that will set the tone of his work: "Truly man is a marvelously vain, diverse, and undulating object. It is hard to found any constant and uniform judgment on him" (I: 1, 5). Hence the basis for paradox, relativism, and mutability is established from the very outset, and the challenge to essaying man, and himself, is sounded.

Similarly the first essay in the second book, "Of the Inconsistency of our Actions," echoes the thematic and structural functions of its counterpart in the first book. Interestingly enough, the first essay of the second book was composed (1572–74) before the first essay of the first book. Again Montaigne points to weakness of judgment in the face of incessant change, but he stresses the theme of man's helplessness which prefigures this essential notion in that book's basic essay, the "Apology of Raymond Sebond":

Our ordinary practice is to follow the inclinations of our appetite, to the left, to the right, uphill and down, as the wind of circumstance carries us. We think of what we want only at the moment we want it, and we change like that animal which takes the color of the place you set it on. What we have just now planned, we presently change, and presently again we retrace our steps: nothing but oscillation and inconsistency . . . . We do not go; we are carried away, like floating objects, now gently, now violently, according as the water is angry or calm. (II: 1, 240)

Then at the end of this essay he proclaims one of the basic tenets of essaying that aims at conquering mutability and inconsistency, and sums up a good deal of the preceding book and becomes a link with it. Contradictions may overwhelm judgment, but they may allow us to discern the core: "a sound intellect will refuse to judge men simply by their outward actions; we must probe the inside and discover what springs set men in motion" (p. 244). Then appears a lurking smile whose purpose is to rock but not overturn a stance taken too overtly: "But since this an arduous and hazardous undertaking, I wish fewer people would meddle with it" (*ibid.*). Yet Montaigne is bold enough to do so!

IV   *From Self-Apology to Self-Assertion*

Thus the first two essays of the first two books offer a variation on themes that mold those books into an integrated whole. This

initial effort, spanning at least eight years, will continue, of course
to have thematic impacts on the third book. But the introductory
essay of the third book, "Of the Useful and the Honorable," bears
a totally different stamp from its two predecessors; it conveys the
sense of a self-apology on the part of Montaigne for choosing to
involve himself in essaying rather than in public life. He had first
retired from the Bordeaux parliament in 1570–71, at the age of
thirty-eight, in order to compose the first two books. Then in 1580–
81 he went on a seventeen-month trip, in Italy, from where he was
called back to become mayor of Bordeaux, a post he held for two
terms until 1585, and which he left ostensibly because of the dangers
of plague and civil war in that city. His contemporaries blamed him
for this act of cowardice, as they thought it; so that when he begins
to write his third book, Montaigne feels the need, more than ever,
to exonerate himself from these accusations: "No one is exempt
from saying silly things. The misfortune is to say them with earnest
effort" (III: 1, 599). Again here is a bitter smile. And he offers as a
challenge to his narrow-minded judges the third book, composed
in hardly more than two years, by one who was by this time master
of the genre.[4] The call to essaying is as much a willful decision as a
divine or fateful ordainment: "We cannot do everything. Do what
we will, we must often commit the protection of our vessel, as to a
sheet anchor, to the guidance of Heaven" (p. 607). Significantly,
the next three essays—that is four out of thirteen—also continue
to weaken this conflict of conscience; "Of Repentance" (III: 2)
denies any need to repent; "Of Three Kinds of Association" (III: 3)
affirms the hegemony of books over association with men or women;
and "Of Diversion" (III: 4) unhesitatingly opts for essaying.
The move from self-apology to self-assertion once and for all
resolves the conflict and confronts the public with the creative
product.

The die then is cast, categorically, both for the present and
retrospectively. Essaying will prevail. There were, there will be,
pitfalls, turned into challenges by Montaigne and into the very
raison d'être of the *Essays*. One such is the vain pursuit of knowledge
resulting from the process of intellectual and philosophical ex-
plorations that deny a system; implicit vainglory; others are the
limits of language and literature, which paradoxically produce a
new genre defying conventional order; and the inherent failure of
self-discovery, liable to the mutability of time; the expression of

positions by accumulation of instances and not by articulation which is soon superseded (hence the superiority of image over rhetoric). A belief in the unlimited may curtail success, but the notion of freedom has dominated thought and action; herein lies the substance of the existential, hedonistic, and creative victory. And the discovery of the measure of Man.

CHAPTER 2

Evolution or Convolution?

WHEN a major critic writes a major study on a major writer, such an endeavor can rejuvenate the subject it deals with, but at the same time it frequently also locks this subject into a critical position for a long time to come, though on the positive side it offers a challenge to future critics. Such has been the effect of Pierre Villey's *Les Sources et l'évolution des Essais de Montaigne.*[1] Villey established that Montaigne's thought evolved through three stages: Stoicism marks the first book; skepticism the second book; naturalism (follow nature) and the goodness of man the third book, while epicureanism pervades all three books. The first question the reader may ask himself is how there can be a conscious and authentic evolution from the first to the second book when many essays in both parts were composed around the same period of time, and Montaigne himself chose to arrange some of his essays more according to thematic patterns than chronologically.

I   *From Stoicism, to Skepticism, to Naturalism?*

Without a doubt these three positions occur in the respective three books; what remains problematic is whether they occupy such a dominating role as to warrant the notion of an evolution. What troubles the reader again is that Montaigne's mind does not function along the lines of fixed patterns that dominate it for extended periods of time. In other words, the very genre of of the essay—weighing, experiment, tryout—does not allow one stance to override another. Of course, in the first book the stoic viewpoint is very clearly and explicitly discernible:

Here very eloquently and fully is that state of the Stoic sage:
The mind remains unmoved, the tears all useless flow.

Virgil

The peripatetic sage does not exempt himself from perturbations, but he moderates them. (I: 12, 31)

The key word here, summing up Montaigne's thinking process, is "Peripatetic" which suggests a circular motion in accord with the exploratory spirit of the essays, and not a linear one more concordant with the concept of evolution. Not adopting any ism may be a wiser device for singling out the highlights of the first book: "Montaigne's problem in the early *Essays* is not merely the human one of seeking happiness in liberation from fear but that of the humanist, who must rise above the common herd by his readiness to meet pain and death like a sage."[2] The lack of a label confers flexibility, and this kind of synthesis remains relative to others and in a global existential perspective.

The second book most readily falls prey to an overriding synthesis because one essay, "Apology of Raymond Sebond," quite centrally situated, dominates the whole book by virtue of constituting more than one-third of it. In this essay Montaigne develops the insufficiency of reason, judgment, and the senses as means to attain knowledge. The result is the renowned "What do I know?" and submission to God. The skepticism inherent in this essay pervades, of course, the entire second book, but it echoes equally strong and convincing notes of the first book, notes that are echoed in the third book as well, because Montaigne's temper is basically skeptic; his questioning mind remains suspended, and he never tires of inquiring. There is a difference of surface stress, of the number of pages devoted explicitly and theoretically to doubt, but the very method of the essay common to all three books results from a skeptical point of departure and arrival.

No one can object to the assertion that following nature and a belief in the natural goodness of man play an important role in the third book. But one may question a critical opinion advocating that Montaigne evolves to this position with the advent of the last book, as Villey proclaimed. To counter this viewpoint, it suffices to take one of the early essays in the first book, "That to Philosophize is to Learn to Die." Here Montaigne wants to relegate to obsolescence man's fear of death and substitute the scorn of death for the scorn of life. All are equal before death, for which we must be ready at any moment. If death spares us until old age, then the sunset years bring a gradually disintegrating body and ease us into the final step. Furthermore, on the threshold of death a man must shed all paraphernalia—the hysterical, mourning relatives, the seemingly concerned preachers and doctors: "We must strip the mask from things as well as from persons; when it is off, we shall find beneath only that same death which a valet or a mere chambermaid passed through not long ago without fear" (I : 20, 68), because "Such are the good counsels of our mother Nature" (p. 67). In the final analysis, Montaigne advocates a simple, natural, and quiet death, one that has become an integral but not an obsessive part of life; of course this ultimate position holds for a death that occurs at home or in old age, not on the field of battle. In the third book Montaigne will take an identical stance.

II   *The Limits of Mutability*

The fact remains that the concept of evolution is endemic to the *Essays*; only the type of evolution may be questioned. And more and more the belief in an evolution of Montaigne's thought has come under fire: "Much, probably far too much, has been made by many a scholar, following Pierre Villey's remarkable study, of the evolution of the essay as practised with growing mastery by Montaigne and the sinuous continuity of Montaigne's thought."[3] In this regard, the growing consensus maintains that Montaigne was not successively a stoic, a skeptic, and finally a naturalist; instead, he was all three at the same time and refused to mold himself into a school of thought. Neither did the means and ends of his attitudes change—his convictions about the relativism of opinions and of ethics fusing with customs, the hegemony of imagination, the inscrutable role of fortune.[4]

One kind of evolution on which no discord exists marks the changing nature of the essay, noted as well by Villey. The first essays consist of examples and anecdotes arranged around a given theme, although each essay contains groups of opposing themes. Perhaps Montaigne at first even had these examples, derived from his reading, before him and then sought to connect them to each other, but surely an awareness of resulting contrasts of concepts provided him with an impetus to write on. In the first essays the example or anecdote may bring about a commentary on it, whereas in later essays it is likely to be present in order to illustrate his thought. The frequency of anecdotes and examples tends to diminish as the essays progress, but not necessarily that of Latin quotations. These have the same metaphoric and didactic purposes as the other means, because Montaigne continues to

need poles of reference against which he can essay, try himself
and the reader out. It is also generally accepted that the early
essays are more impersonal than the later ones; but this sense of
evolution denies the consubstantiality of the *Essays* present from
the very start, that is, the interrelationship and mutual need of
author and his writings. There is, however, a change from an implicit
to a dominating explicit preoccupation with the self. [5]

Other forms of evolution have been suggested, but they remain
open to question. Does the author of the *Essays* move from a role
as writer of a private record for the perusal of relatives and friends,
in the first two books, to thinking of himself as a writer of a book
directed to all mankind? Such a critical opinion assumes the
sincerity of the introductory "To the Reader"—a debatable or
even dubious interpretation.[6] Some observe that the *Essays* evolves
from an awareness that the sum of knowledge is invalid to the
belief in the legitimacy of division and discrimination of knowledge.
The quest, then, has practically no aim except that of a formal
endeavor with an unlimited subject. The resulting shift is from an
essay seen as a totality structured around a theme to an essay that
is a long equivocal and disorganized diversity; in other words,
from an affirmation to a critical analysis of affirmations.[7] Here
one can retort that diversity and critical analysis of affirmations
exist from the very beginning.

One of the more famous statements by Montaigne epitomizes
the notion of mutability which itself would substantiate the
concept of evolution: "I do not portray being: I portray passing"
(III: 2, 611). The limits of this mutability are that becoming does
not lead to being and can never reach it, but on the other hand
being does lead to becoming, which can comprehend both being
and becoming. This revelation or success remains partly thwarted,
however, by a process of incessant change inherent to man. Becoming is an evolution, but a self-destructive one, since no fixed
point can be reached. This particular denial of evolution is applicable
on a more concrete and narrow scale, within an essay itself. A
recent study has shown that in many instances there is no real
difference in meaning between the first edition text of an essay
in the first book and subsequent additions to the same essay in
later years. Although there may be some change in emphasis,
the additions simply develop the argument, but do not alter it.[8]

Ultimately, the concept of evolution, on a thematic level at

least, depends on whether or not Montaigne offers a synthesis
of his thought; if there is no synthesis, then the resulting suspension
of judgment denies any possibility of evolution because a constant
state of ambiguity does not allow for a thematic curve. Under
these circumstances, even the notion of duration, the arching
span of time during which the *Essays* was composed, cannot
substantiate a thematic evolution. Since the general consensus
of opinion now holds that the *Essays* defies synthesis, the belief
in a thematic evolution of Montaigne's thought is accorded less
and less of critical favor. [9]

III   *Ambiguity*

Because Montaigne wants to omit no valid viewpoint, he creates
an ambiguity in his essays; indeed, the reader is at a loss to choose
the validity of one opinion over another. The thorough dissection
of an argument inevitably produces conflicting meanings, since
one is always reversed by another. In the maze of opinions, to
give one a privileged position over another, to consider one a
conclusion or a definitive stance above another, is to fall into a
trap and not discern much tongue-in-cheek aimed at purposely
disconcerting the reader. If one of the aims of the *Essays* is to
form Montaigne's and our judgment, as is unanimously acknow-
ledged, then this goal cannot be achieved by accepting absolutes
or choosing stances, but by weighing arguments—that is, ambivalence and ambiguity. [10]

A close examination of an essay will provide the concrete means
of illustrating a typical case of ambiguity. "A Custom of the Island
of Cea" (II: 3) deals with the question of suicide. It is composed
of a series of examples and anecdotes offering arguments for and
against suicide. The overwhelming bulk of arguments favors it
under some circumstance, such as suffering from some illnesses
(long mental ones or kidney stones) and inevitable loss of honor
or virtue, usually by force. Montaigne even offers the stoics' argument that suicide allows man to remain free and choose, if need be,
a "reasonable exit" (p. 255). On the other hand, one of the fewer
arguments against suicide states that man is not free to dispose
of his life, God's gift to him. The last sentence of the essay, significantly enough a post-1588 addition, indicates that Montaigne
remains consistent between his early and late positions, on the

surface at least: "Unendurable pain and fear of a worse death seem to me the most excusable motives for suicide" (p. 262).

The title of the essay, however, unsettles the underpinning of the synthesis suggested by this consistency. Why does Montaigne call his essay "A Custom of the Island Cea" and choose thereby to focus on a specific example over others? To further stress its importance, not only is it the longest example in the essay, but it occurs at the end of the essay, where its unsettling and destructive effect on what precedes it will be felt more acutely. On that island, "a woman of great authority" who "had spent ninety years in a very happy state of mind and body" (p. 261) decides that the time has come to dispose of her life. She wants all to witness it and proceeds to describe the progress of the poison through her body and takes pleasure in her ability to watch herself die. Although Montaigne has assured the reader previously (I: 20) that a life is long enough wherever it stops, does he not offer here a projection of the death he would like to have—a death that in fact rejects suicide, since it occurs at age ninety and looks back to a long and useful life? In theory, then, Montaigne advocates suicide under certain circumstances, but in practice he denies it and even leads up to rejecting it by implication. In the last analysis he refuses to take a categorical stance on this issue, and many another because "Only the fools are certain and assured" (I: 26, 111).

On occasion Montaigne contrives the end of an essay in such a way as to deliberately pull the rug from under his feet, and thereby contributes to an ambiguity of subject matter. One instance of this technique occurs at the end of the well-known essay "Of Cannibals" (I: 31). Here Montaigne praises the notion of the noble savage and questions the concept of civilization as Western man understands it. He focuses on the cyclical nature of civilization and the superiority of a natural way of life unencumbered by materialism. However, unwilling to find himself out on a limb, he makes one last remark that clouds his earlier perhaps idealistic outlook: "All this is not too bad—but what's the use? They don't wear breeches" (p. 159). It is as if Montaigne built a larger and taller argumentative castle in order to watch it fall, with some glee, from a greater height. He can accept fully neither the noble savage's innocence nor Western man's often corrupt and false well-being; he perceives the good and the bad of both sides.

IV   *Antithesis and Paradox*

Because Montaigne endeavors to show both sides of an argument, or more often its multifaceted complexity, he is constantly confronted with antithesis. He does not flee it, but on the contrary, seeks it out, for it expresses what he reads, experiences, and sees all about him. Of course, what he reads or experiences may conflict with what he sees, or what he sees may contradict his reading, but the convergence of these antitheses provides the impetus to search further, to try again and again, with no hope of arriving at conclusive answers: "My conceptions and my judgment move only by groping, staggering, stumbling, and blundering; and when I have gone ahead as far as I can, still I am not at all satisfied: I can still see country beyond, but with a dim and clouded vision, so that I cannot clearly distinguish it" (I: 26, 107).

The presentation of antithetical patterns of thought does not necessarily reflect belief in a universe hopelessly fragmented and of irreconcilable views. In Montaigne's mind opposites coexist, reinforce each other, and actually harmonize into a composite flexible whole. At the same time, one finds in the *Essays* a series of opposites: a love of life and a detachment from it, hedonism and heroism, an acceptance of the principle of becoming and an aspiration toward constancy and serenity, the eventual failure of thought before the vastness of knowledge, or an intellectual humility, and yet a limitless pride and conviction of the hegemony of thought (a variant of the Pascalian reed), virtue emanating both from spontaneous and rational sources and inherent to our nature, the dichotomy of the artful and the natural, the conscious and the subconscious. I cite only a few. On a smaller scale, the reader will often encounter antithesis on the paragraph level. Here Montaigne will start the argument along one line of thought and will surreptitiously lead the reader to the opposite viewpoint without realizing it, until he finds himself on the other side of the argument and often equally convinced of both. The use of the antithesis mystifies the reader and toys with him; black and white fuse into a grey zone. It may produce surprise, but more important, one consequence of Montaigne's antinomism or dualism is that it is unwise to make any statement about him without immediately stating the contrary.[11]

The paradox is the most intensive form of antithesis because the weighing process disappears; instead, the result turns out to be the opposite of the avowed purpose of the argument. It constitutes a challenge to thought and appeals therefore to the humanistic mind. The Renaissance relishes the paradox, because this device reflects the infinity and inscrutability of knowledge constantly faced by the humanist.[12] At the same time, paradox becomes one of the few reliable means of arriving at a perplexing and elusive truth. Thus Montaigne likes to take the counterpoint of an argument. In discussing education, he pictures himself unworthy of tackling such a subject matter; this kind of reasoning is one of his favorite ploys to draw the reader to his side. He creates a hesitant, unpresumptuous persona for himself, to attack and sometimes praise presumption. He devotes a whole essay to repentance, and in it advocates nonrepentance. His treatise on friendship sees the complete transformation of this concept into that of love, and conjugal love in his eyes becomes friendship. Desires, passions, anger, fright form the very core for opposite themes such as moderation, ataraxy (complete spiritual quietude), sleep, death, reconciliation. Neither moderation nor excess are ever exempt from incertitude and inquietude; therefore the questioning, the essay, continues. The oscillation persists: "Wisdom has its excesses, and has no less need of moderation than does folly" (III: 5, 639).[13] The paradox, then, is to be seen as a positive device, because the need to surprise that it supplies is less important than the apparent negation of the accepted ordinary in order to explore and reevaluate.[14]

When Montaigne decides to take a stance, he does so temporarily in a single matter and for a single moment. The paradoxes derive from a dialectical process inherent to the *Essays*, namely, from the relationship, the movement between his readings and his experiences, between his ideas and other people's, the perpetual dialogue within himself, between him and his book, between the past, the present, and himself. This constant interchange, what Montaigne calls the pouring out and the filling, remains at a loose equilibrium and culminates in the last essay, "Of Experience" (III: 13), which combines reading and experience, the past and the present, into an entity based as well on the interdependence of these elements. Again the presence of a paradoxical and dialectical thinking process effects and may even negate the concept of an evolution.

V *Mobilism: Linear, Vertical, Inner-Outer*

No one denies the presence and importance of the notion of movement in the *Essays*, but its relation to their evolution remains problematic. Montaigne himself asserts incessantly the dominance of movement within and about him. In the *Essays* there are three dimensions of this phenomenon: linear or horizontal, vertical, and inner-outer. The linear dimension is usually referred to as Bergsonian mobilism, an expression derived from the precepts of the modern French philosopher Henri Bergson. He held that time, the idea of duration, is composed of moments. Since time is infinite and moments are finite, the latter could take precedence in the search for stability or an absolute. However, since a moment represents only a point in a certain space and time, it becomes relative, if not obsolete, in the face of another moment taken at another phase of time and space. Duration, then, is the sum of everchanging components. Furthermore, the very notion of duration is itself nothing more than a fragment, a moment, of a larger whole beyond man's conception. As a result, mutability and inconstancy dominate Bergsonian mobilism, and the outer stability and constancy will remain elusive.[15]

Seen in the light of Bergsonian mobilism, each essay is a moment in a duration, the *Essays*. Although each essay contains contradictions within itself, the result of experiences of the moment, it still represents the creative product at a certain point in time and space, but to be enlarged upon and supplanted by the next essay. Taken as a whole, then, the essays contrast with each other as well as within a single one, and it is the notion of mutability that causes conflicting views: "The world is but a perennial movement. All things in it are constant motion . . . both with the common motion and with their own. Stability itself is nothing but a more languid motion" (III: 2, 610). This cosmic condition produces what in French is referred to as *inscience* or "unknowledge." This state of constant flux makes man helpless in the realm of assured knowledge.

On the surface, Bergsonian mobilism seems to follow a linear course, but such a movement implies a point of departure and a reached destination. Since this pattern constitutes the exception more than the rule, on the level of knowledge of things, people, ethics, and metaphysics, the perceptual line of thought assumes a curve around the subject discussed. The aim of a discussion is to explore all the facets of the matter from as many vantage points as possible in time and space, to bring to bear on the arguments opinions from the past and the present and from different countries and civilizations. The result is a prismatic view of the subject very much like a cubist painting or like the characterization of a Swann, for example, made later by Proust, Montaigne's spiritual heir. The process of thinking does not progress as we usually understand it, but instead gravitates and plunges back within itself. The vocabulary to express this peripatetic motion derives indeed from the realm of walking, an active motion, or from following footsteps, a passive one; the interaction of the two keeps the intellect in ferment. However, this peripatetic intellectual motion assumes the role of kinetic activity that satisfies itself, that wanders and meanders for the pleasure of doing so; according to some, the process of exploration may even prevail over the achievement.[16]

The vertical movement operates in function of Montaigne's self; it consists of an oscillation of that self between a high and a low position in relation to others. Montaigne sees himself and presents himself either above or beneath other men, but never quite on the same level. More frequently he prefers to set himself beneath others, but in the process he turns out to be above them. He takes the low road, he creates an inferior image of himself, in order to indulge in a high game of intellectual juggling and to arrive at a middle position between the average man and the vulgar, wisdom and ignorance, religion and social behavior. By the same token, from a lofty position he aims for a low one; since the former supposes an ascending motion, he will choose to bring himself down. He turns the ordinary thinking cap inside out. His model, actually the metaphor and projection of himself, is Socrates, who epitomizes Montaigne's own kinetic mode of thinking:

Socrates makes his soul move with a natural and common motion. So says a peasant, so says a woman. His mouth is full of nothing but carters, joiners, cobblers, and masons. His are inductions and similes drawn from the commonest and best-known actions of men; everyone understands him. Under so mean a form we should never have picked out the nobility and splendor of his admirable ideas, we who consider flat and low all ideas that are not raised up by learning, and who perceive richness only in pomp and show. Our world is formed only for ostentation; men inflate themselves only with wind, and go bouncing around like balls. This man did not propose to himself any idle fancies: his aim was to furnish us with things and precepts that serve life really and more closely:

To keep the mean, to hold our aim in view,
And follow nature.
— *Lucan*

He was always one and the same, and raised himself, not by sallies but by disposition, to the utmost point of vigor. Or, to speak more exactly, he raised nothing, but rather brought vigor, hardships, and difficulties down and back to his own natural and original level, and subjected them to it. (III: 12, 793)

In fact, the purpose of the ascending movement is to return to the point of departure a bit more assured than before; change really does not take place: "He was always one and the same." Only the residual sediments from this vertical movement become more apparent to Montaigne and the reader, after repeated efforts.

The inner-outer movement reflects a sharp division between a steady inner core of the self and an inconstant and false appearance of the self. Although he seeks, praises, and falls back repeatedly on the former, Montaigne still has to live with the masks, his included, that all wear in spite of his intense criticism of this exterior sham. As a result, throughout the *Essays* he alternates between the two, opposing one to the other: "We must play our part duly, but as the part of a borrowed character. Of the mask and appearance we must not make a real essence, nor of what is foreign what is our very own. We cannot distinguish the skin from the shirt. It is enough to make up our face, without making up our heart" (III: 10, 773). Montaigne accepts the impurity of the outer human shell because he knows that the inner self composed of a controlled will and moderation, remains constant and actually profits from exposures to the mutable exterior. In fact, the hard inner core tests itself and exposes itself by means of confrontations with the outer self, a reflection of the outside world.

One constant that pervades the *Essays*, then, is the one of the inner self, unflaunted but enriched by experiences with an inconstant outer self; this interaction becomes a necessity for the very creation of the essays. One result of this kind of movement is an alternation between a reaching out that broadens oneself and the inevitable falling back upon oneself that offers a degree of security, but restricts and narrows the field of visibility. On the other hand, the outer self and the outside world present a constant. What

Montaigne refers to as the "human condition," the contradictions of life and the inevitable death, does not change and continues to challenge man. Furthermore, the mutability of the outer self and of the outside world is a constant itself with which Montaigne becomes reconciled. Indeed, one can live with constancy only in terms of inconstancy, or rather when constancy is immanent to inconstancy because one exists in function of the other. The cessation of the interplay between the two brings intellectual death. Hence the incessant movement between the immutable spiritual core, being, and the evanescent outer world and outside world, seeming— actually a creative friction between two constants, in Montaigne's eyes.

VI *Evolutions of Form*

Two matters affecting the formal composition of the *Essays* have traditionally been associated with their evolution: the additions that Montaigne made in later editions to the text of the original editions, and a change in the length of the essays between the first and the last books. Indeed, a number of essays in the first two books are only a page or two long, but their relative shortness is actually quite deceptive for they still exhibit a richness and complexity worthy of longer ones. The vast majority, however, comprise five, six, seven, up to twenty pages and more. And not to be overlooked, of course, is the fact that the second book contains the longest essay of them all, the "Apology of Raymond Sebond," composed over a period of five years (1575–80) and numbering from one hundred to two hundred pages depending on the edition used. Then one points to the longer essays of the third book. True, three out of the thirteen essays comprised by this book number thirty to fifty or more pages. But the remaining ten essays number from fifteen to twenty-five pages or so each. In other words, a lengthening of essays does occur between the first two books and the third in that the essays of two or three pages disappear, but the last book is not made up of consistently long essays. It is perhaps a new way of working for Montaigne, because when he wrote the very short essays he also composed long ones. Thus the shortness of an essay does not necessarily reflect an incapacity to compose on a larger scale or a lack of inspiration, but a choice on Montaigne's part to limit the discussion, to explore within a limited spatial frame, but not within a more limited thematic one.

The usual assumption about the additions to the text is that they would indicate a change of position over a period of time, an evolution of thought. The first additions occur in the 1588 edition of the *Essays* which includes the third book for the first time; they are made to the essays of the first two books only, and in most modern editions a "b" marks the beginning of this layer of additions. Then a "c" indicates those made between 1588 and 1592, which appeared in the posthumous edition (1595). Surprisingly enough, Villey, the ardent advocate of an evolution, downgrades and even disparages the additions; he asserts that the essays have lost much of their clarity because of these additions and have also taken on an air of pedantry.[17] Villey has failed to see their function of adding dimensions to an argument in time and space. He does free himself of any possible negative judgments by professing not to indulge in literary criticism, but history.

Some of the additions to the first two books in the 1588 edition form veritable excrescenses upon the original text; these are much longer than any found in the 1595 edition. There is one, for example, in the "Apology for Raymond Sebond" that is longer than the shortest essay of the third book.[18] Contrary to what one may surmise, however, the additions, whether they be long or short, do not substantially alter the tenor of the argument. When Montaigne rereads himself, he casts a different light on the subject matter; through additional anecdotes or examples he broadens the scope of the problem posed originally; as he himself puts it: "I add, but I do not correct" (III: 9, 736). Actually, when he returns to a topic, Montaigne does not wish to contradict what he wrote earlier, but simply to elaborate on the divergent views already present in the original text. Thus he remains faithful to a position taken at a certain point in time and space even though later, or in the very same essay, he will offer an opposing opinion. As a result, the spiritual crisis of the "Apology" dominated by skepticism does not hinder him from recognizing the validity of views expressed in the first book; by the same token, this crisis was not necessarily overcome when Montaigne began to write the third book. Indeed, it continues in the last book even if "Our great and glorious masterpiece is to live appropriately" (III: 13, 851). Thus the additions to the third book amplify on this art of living, but without losing sight of a pervading intellectual crisis—or probably because of it.[19]

In an addition of the last stratum, post-1588, Montaigne can therefore unabashedly proclaim the integrity of his work in spite of the numerous additions that may seem to distort the thought and the text: "My book is always one. Except that at each new edition, so that the buyer may not come off completely empty-handed, I allow myself to add, since it is only an ill-fitted patchwork, some extra ornaments. These are only overweights, which do not condemn the original form, but give some special value to each of the subsequent ones, by a bit of ambitious subtlety" (III: 9. 736). If one accepts the amplifying function of the additions, then the notion of a thematic evolution loses further ground.

However, seen in a certain light, the concept of evolution remains perfectly valid. On a stylistic level, for example, it has been noted that word pairs, the accumulation of two words or more having a synonymous or conflicting meaning, occur for the most part after 1580. As a matter of fact, they occur far more frequently in the third book and in the additions after 1588, and an element of strangeness or surprise is more clearly present. In addition, the more elaborate, intricate, and interesting combinations of these word pairs tend to come in the later stages, namely, in the third book and after 1588.[20] Transposed to the thematic plane, this stylistic evolution would indicate that Montaigne to the very last and more than ever stresses diversity, paradox, and antithesis.

VII   *The Pervading Self*

The one explicitly pervading element in the *Essays* is the self and its study by Montaigne. Since this self-observation lasted about twenty years, it can be assumed that the "I" underwent some changes. On the most obvious plane, it evolved from a middle-aged man to an old one; consequently, the last essays do exhibit a dominant preoccupation with old age and a decaying body, yet one of the early essays, "Of Age" (I: 57), written when Montaigne was in his late thirties, already reflects and projects a latent obsession with this question. In a more subtle vein, the self moves from a "diverse and undulating" being in the first essays, the very condition leading to the act of writing, toward a formed and fixed being, but one who still seeks for self-definition. In other words, Montaigne tries out stability just as he had tried out and parried with vacillation earlier.[21] In the process, he moves from being a mere borrower to becoming a proprietor of the past, of his sources, and of himself, as he proceeds to an unattainable future. What matters to the "I" is the present, the only temporal phase that can be ordered, created, and lived. Given this premise, the self feels the oppression and limitations of time from which its consciousness emerges.[22] This awareness makes the self live time and thereby conquer it, the purpose of the *Essays*. From the beginning to the end of his writings, Montaigne points to the supremacy of living, the existence of the self, and the integration of the self with his environment and with the *Essays*.

"My trade and my art is living" (II: 6, 274). Although this assertion occurs in one of the earlier essays, it is actually a post-1588 addition found in an essay that advocates "practicing" death; sleep or fainting simulates death, but in the final analysis only through living, through actions do we overcome it. However, the activity advocated foremost by Montaigne is the study of the self, and therefore in this same essay, when coming back to it, he adds several pages that constitute the end, glorifying a growing observation of the self as the best means of learning how to die and overcome death:

It is many years now that I have had only myself as object of my thoughts, that I have been examining and studying only myself; and if I study anything else, it is in order promptly to apply it to myself, or rather within myself. And it does not seem to me that I am making a mistake if—as is done in the other sciences, which are incomparably less useful—I impart what I have learned in this one, though I am hardly satisfied with the progress I have made in it. There is no description equal in difficulty, or certainly in usefulness, to the description of oneself. Even so one must spruce up, even so one must present oneself in an orderly arrangement, if one would go out in public. Now I am constantly adorning myself, for I am constantly describing myself. . . . I expose myself entire: my portrait is a cadaver on which the veins, the muscles, and the tendons appear at a glance, each part in its place. One part of what I am was produced by a cough, another by a pallor or a palpitation of the heart—in any case dubiously. It is not my deeds that I write down; it is myself, it is my essence. [273, 274]

Although this self-scrutiny becomes more and more introspective, the body as whole is at the same time agent and instrument. Indeed, Montaigne takes pleasure in rolling himself within himself like a twirling ball, for it is through this action that he defines himself, not so much through the amount or nature of the space explored as through the energy expended in the exploration of the self. This energy alternates between an active and a passive self, between initiating and sustaining; even in the latter role the object is to remain a free agent, to be able to resist if the choice so warrants it.[23] The involvement with oneself operates on the same bilevel as the involvement with the outside world.

As the essays progress and old age sets in, Montaigne exhibits more and more intimate details about himself. The wines and dishes he likes or does not like; those he used to enjoy and can no longer have now. The loss of a tooth, his bowel movements, his kidney stones, matters with which he becomes more and more obsessed. These personal preoccupations, less frequent in the first essays than in the last, do mark a movement of the *Essays* toward an interior physiological level that functions in the light of living in harmony with oneself: "The most beautiful lives, to my mind, are those that conform to the common human pattern, with order, but without miracle and without eccentricity" (III: 13, 857). Shifts here and there of details do not alter the main thrust of the essays: the analysis of the self.

On the surface it appears that the essays evolve from an impersonal to a personal level, from the outside world, being in function of the inner self, toward a fusion of the outside and personal worlds in function of the inner self, but this kind of evolution does not take into account the all-pervading consubstantiality throughout the three books. Yet a perceptible movement toward a narrower and narrower self who at the same time claims world citizenship and universality (cf. III: 9, 766) remains one of the more evident and plausible—indeed, paradoxical—evolutions. The individual looking at the outside world becomes the prototype looking inside of himself. The more Montaigne wraps himself up with himself, the more aware he becomes of his universality; convolution produces nakedness and unveils a "ruling pattern" (III: 2, 615), the growing inner core that resists mutation but profits from experiences and essaying because, in spite of appearances, man carries on "all in one piece" (p. 616).

CHAPTER 3

Searching, Discovering, Writing

THE *Essays* poses a fundamental existential question: How should man confront the adversities of life and deal with the human condition? It is no accident that the very first essay, "By Diverse Means We Arrive at the Same End," posits metaphorically this philosophical reality and offers what will become the usual fluid answer: "The commonest way of softening the hearts of those we have offended, when, vengeance in hand, they hold us at their mercy, is by submission to move them to commiseration and pity. However, audacity and steadfastness—entirely contrary means —have sometimes served to produce the same effect" (I: 1,3). Should man endure, hoping for the best, or should he resist and stand up to his existential situation? If success can be realized either through submission or through involvement, it always implies a previous participation in a battle, a state of consciousness. As a matter of fact, the anecdotes and examples found in many an essay of the first two books depict a battle situation and a protagonist's behavior surrounding it. Man, then, is cast in both a passive and an active role, with no clear distinction between the two because of the impossibility of knowing which may be the best in a given instance and because Montaigne will reverse and purposely confuse the usually accepted meanings of these words. Action therefore is never questioned, but its nature is; and excess is always condemned, as witnessed at the end of the same first essay in the case of Alexander's bloody cruelty toward those who resist him and exhibit steadfastness.

I *The Existential Temper*

On the surface, stoicism could appear under the guise of a passivity, but what appealed to Montaigne in this ideological framework is the choice of the time of death made by the individual and the serenity with which the stoic lives and awaits death. Choice (which entails freedom of action) and serenity (the reflection of an inner constancy) remain Montaigne's ideals throughout the *Essays*. Cato the Younger, ordinarily associated with stoicism, embodies these qualities, but the references to him in the first two books— a whole essay is even devoted to him (I: 37)—do not necessarily imply an adherence to stoicism. Socrates, for example, reflects just as strongly these ideals; his presence throughout and especially toward the end of the *Essays* could equally well indicate a stoic position. The fact of the matter is, however, that both these personalities circumvent any attempt to subsume them under any label, for they embody the virtues that Montaigne has always clung to. Seneca; another adherent of the Stoic school, also has his place in the *Essays*, but we concur with the opinion that Montainge admires him more for his psychological insights into human conduct than for his philosophical notions.[1] If one accepts these premises about Cato and Seneca, for example, it follows that Montaigne's stoicism is more of a literary than a personal nature; that is, stoicism does not reflect doctrinal convictions, but is rather used at given times to fit the argument presented.[2] And the existential framework transcends the stoic elements, supporting a broader ideological stance.

A basic enterprise of the *Essays* is Montaigne's endeavor to find out how to live and how to die; the two are inextricably intertwined. The search for the self operates in function of this enterprise and reveals therefore the existential thread throughout the three books. Montaigne asks the two questions repeatedly, and offers a variety of answers due to the skepticism that permeates his thought processes. The final solution, that he offers at the very end of the essays, namely, a reconciliation with oneself, does not take into account the inconsistencies and contradictions of knowledge itself and of the outside physical and social world. In other words, he does not resolve the dilemma of skepticism; he obviates it without rejecting it because the validity of self-knowledge, the inside world, remains steadfast only if one accepts the incongruities of the outside world.

Although skepticism per se abounds in negative connotations, critics rightfully point out its positive value in Montaigne's thought. Skepticism, more than an argument, shakes it thoroughly, and in the process questions accepted norms. Doubt, then, becomes a longing for the absolute.[3] It creates a certain equilibrium of varied tendencies and of contradictory opinions that oppose and neutralize each other; in the process, however, this equilibrium brings back to the fore the ambiguous diversity of opinions. Skepticism,

or Pyrrhonism, can also be seen in the light of mobilism or mutability; then it reflects a continuous flux of judgment that stresses
the concept of a lasting change and the plurality of philosophies.[4]
It leads to an endless quest for knowledge, and, in the case of
Montaigne, not necessarily a quest for God, since it depicts the
adventures of the mind, not the soul. A skeptic will end up accepting
the superiority of the pure appearance of things and will derive
from it an enriching experience because of the changing and diverse
nature of appearances. Since Pyrrhonism produces a suspension
of judgment, an inability to choose between two or more equally
valid opinions, it becomes a therapeutic philosophy that cures man
of a swollen imagination and attempts to restore him to his natural
common sense.[5] Yet the quest itself contains inherently a measure
of vanity never quite overcome; otherwise the search for knowing
would cease. Hence this particular purgative capability of skepticism
does have some limits.[6]

Although skepticism denies any pretense toward knowledge,
it asserts in a rightful claim that it forges the mind by exposing
the latter to varying and conflicting arguments. This creative function of skepticism has a more significant impact on the *Essays*
than the purgative one observed by the ancients. In this context,
Pyrrhonism has a direct effect on the self-discovery process; it
contributes to the creation of the self by the transfiguration of a
rich and fluid knowledge. Skepticism, then, does not produce
despair or a feeling of the absurd; on the contrary, it constitutes a
basic ingredient of the self-consciousness toward which Montaigne
strives. The famous *Que sçai-je?* (What do I know?) of Montaigne
does not imply therefore a spiritual floundering and helplessness
in the face of adversity. The speck that he is will assert and adapt
himself to the exigencies of existence while keeping a low profile
strengthened by a strong backbone, unlike Pascal's reed which
wallows in uncertainty and is roughly tossed about in doubt's
boundless sea until fished out by God.

The positive implications of skepticism are reinforced by Montaigne's relatively helpless condition before fate, a condition shared
by all humanists. As a matter of fact, the humanist's attempts to
reconcile religion and fate, to explain catastrophic events or accidents
of life as acts or momentary lapses of a benevolent God, do not
always make sense. Furthermore, the humanist sees in fate an
element which he cannot control, which deprives him of his self-

assertive powers and takes away his dignity, emasculates him. Thus the existence of fate with its unexpected and arbitrary maleficent effects contributes directly to a skeptic and fluid frame of mind. But this very Pyrrhonic attitude also becomes the yeasty ingredient that raises Montaigne toward self-knowledge and thereby helps him break through fortune's constraints. Action helps to overcome fate, and this endless pursuit of knowledge and self-knowledge is the form of activity that will overcome the fortuitous nature of fortune.

The one obsessing fate that man knows he will meet is death, and this one Montaigne succeeds in overwhelming by transforming it into a strong conviction in life while awaiting the inevitable. Although at one point he suggests that a meaningful and dignified death judges ultimately the temper of life (cf. "That Our Happiness Must Not Be Judged Until After Our Death," I: 19), and although man must learn to domesticate death, to grow accustomed to it (cf. "That to Philosophize Is to Learn to Die," I: 20), ultimately a productive life makes death acceptable and less formidable, a natural outcome of the movement of life. Even in the first two positions the importance of living life is not denied. The plenitude of life, usually associated with the third book, surfaces more readily when Montaigne has made peace with himself and reached a state of inner freedom:

As for me, I love life and cultivate it just as God has been pleased to grant it to us. I do not go about wishing that it should lack the need to eat and drink, and it would seem to me no less excusable a failing to wish that need to be doubled. *The wise man is the keenest searcher for natural treasures* [Seneca]. Nor do I wish that we should sustain ourselves by merely putting into our mouths a little of that drug by which Epimenides took away his appetite and kept himself alive; not that we should beget children insensibly with our fingers and heels; not that the body should be without desire and without titillation. (III: 13, 854–55)

This plenitude of life may border on voluptuousness, but essentially it belongs to the realm of the exploration of life, just as valid as the exploration of death and of the mind, and always in the light of reflection and moderation. It inserts itself in the quest for the confusion and meaning of existence, a basic premise of the *Essays*. To avoid any confusion of priorities, the nod is given to the mind, but this hierarchical distinction is quantitative rather than qualitative when Montaigne speaks for Socrates and himself: "He prizes bodily pleasure as he should, but he prefers that of the mind, as having more power, constancy, ease, variety, and dignity. The latter by no means goes alone, according to him—he is not so fanciful—but only comes first. For him temperance is the moderator, not the adversary of pleasure" *(ibid.)*.

II   *Nature and Art*

To live fully but moderately finds its counterpart in living artfully but naturally. The concept of nature occupies an important place in Montaigne's thought because it fits in with his affinity for the spontaneous, the simple, the good, the unspoiled, the humane, the free, the healthy, the varied. On the other hand, the artful to him is synonymous with the artificial, with affected language, conduct, and thought (of the pseudophilosophers), with man-made laws, civilization, social facade, the travails of the imagination. Of course, this dichotomy of art and nature is not always clearly marked; one may even fuse into the other, or the two at times may become interchangeable. This willful confusion and reversability should not surprise, since it concurs with Montaigne's paradoxical and mutable frame of mind. Furthermore, the concept of nature is not a precise one. For example, what does "to follow nature" mean?[7]

Although Montaigne's attitude toward nature seems to follow a curve toward a complete and unchallenging submission to this concept, his position remains ambiguous. In one of the first essays, "Of Cannibals," his admiration for the noble savage, man in his natural state, is not without reservations; he questions, for example, the savages' cruelty, not unlike Western man's, and he condemns their inherent desire to break down their prisoners, to take away their human dignity, their sacred uniqueness. Even the sharp distinction between art and nature in this essay, in spite of its black-and-white presentation, does not deal with the implied positive challenge: "All things, says Plato, are produced by nature, fortune, or by art; the greatest and most beautiful by one or the other of the first two, the least and most imperfect by the last" (p. 153). But the *Essays* itself stands as a contradictory monument to this assertion. Where does art begin and artifice end? Montaigne stands against artifice when it supposes excess and affectation, but the line of demarcation between this artifice and art is not clear at all times. Even the *Essays* could fall prey to being categorized as artifice, in this sense; and Montaigne knows it and laments these so-called weaknesses. But are these complaints genuine, or mere mystifications addressed to the reader?

Although Montaigne seeks spiritual security and eventually finds it, his success is more apparent than real, more outward than inwardly substantial. At the end of the essays, his submission to nature is due as much to a reconciliation with himself as to a condition forced on him by old age. Furthermore, total submission to a dogma or school of thought is quite foreign to him. Thus his adherence to nature may be complete as far as the outer self is concerned, but since the inner spiritual core must at all times exhibit self-balance and control outer forces, it is difficult to believe that this naturalism overwhelms him to the extent that it appears to do on the surface:

> The philosophers with much reason refer us to the rules of Nature: but these have no concern with such sublime knowledge. The philosophers falsify them and show us the face of nature in too high a color, and too sophisticated, whence spring so many varied portraits of so uniform a subject. As she furnished us with feet to walk with, so she has given us wisdom to guide us in life: a wisdom not so ingenious, robust, and pompous as that of their invention, but correspondingly easy and salutary, performing very well what the other talks about, in a man who has the good fortune to know how to occupy himself simply and in an orderly way, that is to say, naturally. The more simply we trust Nature, the more wisely we trust to her. Oh, what a sweet and soft and healthy pillow is ignorance and incuriosity, to rest a well-made head! (III: 13, 821–22)

The point is precisely that Montaigne will not accept unconsciousness and ignorance if naturalism becomes an easy way out. By the same token, he will not accept either a totally falsified nature, that is, artifice. The moderate, intermediate position is the answer, but its exact location is not objectively pinpointed, since it lies relativistically within each one of us.

In the *Essays* the concept of nature has definitely a positive connotation; it conveys a sense of the robust, the mysterious, the creative. On the other hand, art does not carry a totally negative meaning—on the contrary, even though artifice remains more unacceptable because of its affected and distorted composition. In fact, man has the power to transform the natural into the artful or the artificial. However, between nature and art Montaigne creates a gray zone accepting or rejecting neither but attracted by both: "If I were of the trade, I would naturalize art as much as they artify nature" (III: 5, 666). Montaigne's dependency on both nature and art and the actual fusion of the two typify his position throughout the *Essays* and can be seen early in one of the short ones (about two pages long), "Of Smells" (I: 55).[8] Here he begins by saying that smells exist in order to cover up some natural fault. He then declares that the most simple and natural smells are the most agreeable to him. Finally he pits himself against the foul odors and the mud of Paris and Venice "which weaken my fondness for them" (p. 229), but they are still among his favorites. And he likes culinary odors. All in all, good and bad odors, natural and artificial smells blend into a complementary and varied existence.

Whether the concept of nature appears under the guise of a philosophical abstraction, a sensory experience, or an aesthetic criterion, it is ultimately reduced to Montaigne's self as a guideline to living and writing. Learning how to live, however, comes only after learning how to die. And nature ultimately also provides the means of reconciliation toward death, although throughout Montaigne's creative life death remains an obsession. Of the several deaths about him that marked Montaigne's spirit, that of his beloved friend Etienne de La Boétie in 1563 had the most impact on him and eventually became an impulse to write the *Essays* as a memorial to this loss. A few years later his father died in 1568, then his brother at the age of twenty-three, and finally five of his six children. The death of dear ones made him aware of it, but the transition from abstraction to reality occurs most vividly when it is applied to him-himself. Montaigne is obsessed by death not only because he witnesses it about him, but also because he knows he will die himself and wants to find a way to reconcile himself to it and accept it. Furthermore, like most humanists, he is led by this consciousness of death to endeavor to leave a trace behind him, the *Essays*.

III *Death*

Montaigne constantly practices, essays, death; he comprehends what being dead is, but not as well as dying, except in the sense that living is an irreversible manner of dying. His closest personal acquaintance with the act of dying is a long fainting spell as a result of a fall from a horse; a whole essay is devoted to this experience, "Of Practice" (II: 6). In fact, he discusses much more the ideal death in terms of himself than an actual death over whose circumstances he may not have any control; yet "We must be always booted and ready to go, so far as it is in our power" (I: 20, 61). Again Montaigne posits two contradictory stances and places himself between them; one derives rationally from facing a stark reality, and the other arrived at through an idealized position which he hopes to reach. The first one negates the principle of practicing, getting accustomed, to death and at the same time makes this activity more challenging and necessary: "But for dying, which is the greatest task we have to perform, practice cannot help us. A man can, by habit and experience, fortify himself against pain, shame, indigence, and such other accidents; but as for death, we can try it only once: we are all apprentices when we come to it" (II: 6, 267).

The second stance advocates facing death, however, and masticating it in order to ingest it more easily; this position is cast in an admiring framework, and Socrates, Montaigne's hero, is the model to emulate: "There is nothing, in my opinion, more illustrious in the life of Socrates than having had thirty whole days to ruminate his death sentence, having digested it all that time with a very certain expectation, without emotion, without alteration, and with a tenor of actions and words rather lowered and relaxed than strained and exalted by the weights of such a reflection" (II: 13, 461).[9] Of course, by implication, the *Essays* constitutes this "rumination" and Montaigne aims at being as successful as Socrates.

The crux of Montaigne's attitude toward death lies in the distinction between death and dying as it relates to human existence. Life is like going to an inevitable execution. Most rush toward this end because they consciously remain unconscious toward death. To those "Being dead does not trouble them, but dying does indeed" (II: 13, 460). To consider death, then, to take time to think about it, is to slow down its arrival, within a mental temporal framework. Death, therefore, is absence of consciousness, while dying is consciousness; the former implies submission, and the latter spiritual freedom. Since, in this light, dying becomes the essence of living, Montaigne can rightfully assert, "My trade and my art is living" (II: 61 274); needless to say, he means writing the *Essays* as well.

Montaigne faces and explores the options open to him in the process of how to die: suicide, entering forays of battle (that is, involvement), and submission, but in a studied way. Although the first alternative offers freedom of action, he rejects it because, even in the face of adversity, life always has a more meaningful potential. He has tried the second option on the literal level, participation in the affairs of his region, and found the results limited and constraining. Therefore, writing the *Essays* will be a much more worthwhile endeavor and involvement. The first two options reflect the thinking of a younger man bent on acquiring a resolute consciousness of death and on overcoming the fright it inspires.

As he grows older, the third option becomes almost inevitable, and actually, old age leaves him no choice. Acceptance of life, of course, is not helpless resignation but willful control and observation. Then a shift occurs from writing about the dying of others to the analysis of Montaigne's own dying. This self-scrutiny leads to a praxis of life. Montaigne will find the wisdom of dying within himself and by looking at the temporal curve of his life. From the observation of the past to the present and the ensuing gradual decay of the body, he realizes that fright, apprehension, or scorn of death have become useless in the face of the continuum of life. One constant that remains unshaken is a strong will not to relinquish any habits dealing with the sensual enjoyments of life, limited though they may have become. Having arrived at a relatively old age now, he will allow himself to be led, but with his eyes wide open:

Let us see how, in those ordinary changes and declines that we suffer, nature hides from us the sense of our loss and decay. What has an old man left of the vigor of his youth, and of his past life? . . . If we fell into such a change suddenly, I don't think we could endure it. But, when we are led by Nature's hand down a gentle and virtually imperceptible slope, bit by bit, one step at a time, she rolls us into this wretched state and makes us familiar with it; so that we feel no shock when youth dies within us, which in essence and in truth is a harder death than the complete death of a languishing life or the death of old age . . . (I: 19, 63)

Montaigne's final position is a submission to death when it will come and to life as long as it lasts, but the real import of this theme in the *Essays* is his discovery of life in the face of dying—not death.[10] Experience and reason produce such a position. A shift occurs from an obsession with death, when a middle-aged man, to an obsession with life in old age.

IV *Religion and the "Apology for Raymond Sebond"*

The all-pervasiveness of the theme of death in the *Essays* is directly related to religion and may even act as a surrogate for it. This omnipresence of death explains a comment by a critic who understood Montaigne well, to the effect that he who does not place among the foremost problems of Montaigne criticism the religious problem does not understand Montaigne.[11] The validity of such an assertion, however, does not help in deciphering the question. Indeed, Montaigne's religion has lent itself to several conflicting interpretations. This contrast of critical opinions should not surprise, since it reflects an exploring mind typical of the Renaissance.

In trying to assess Montaigne's religion, one would like to refer to the frequency of biblical citations as a possible evaluating guideline, but there are only four in the entire *Essays*. It becomes quite logical, then, to speak of an almost complete absence of the Scriptures in the *Essays,* although such an absence has little bearing on whether Montaigne was religious or not; however, their heavy presence would help toward the definition of religious affinities at certain moments of his spiritual development. Furthermore, references to Christ are very few, and to God quite generic. Interestingly enough, a major source of biblical quotations is found inscribed on the beams of Montaigne's library, seventeen out of a total of fifty-seven; and twelve of the seventeen derive from Ecclesiastes, four from the Pauline books, and one from Proverbs. These quotations stress man's relative weakness and insignificance, his vanity, the difficulty of attaining knowledge and wisdom. It should be noted that Montaigne alters the wording of a good many. The original "Be not over much wicked, neither be thou foolish" (Eccl. 7. 17) becomes "Do not be wiser than necessary in order not to be stupid."[12] It soon appears evident that these scriptural citations substantiate more basic tenets of Montaigne's philosophical thought than the religious one.

However, it is precisely because they reflect Montaigne's framework of thought that these inscriptions, both religious and lay, are important. Transferred to the religious plane, these tenets of fundamental beliefs, namely man's insignificant position in the universe, and the limits of his knowledge, reveal and corroborate Montaigne's own brand of fideism, which is a submission to the

Faith while maintaining the right to question its dogmas. Indeed, Montaigne regards his Christianity as an accident of time and space: "All this is a very evident sign that we receive our religion only in our own way and with our own hands, and not otherwise than as other religions are received. We happen to have been born in a country where it was in practice; or we regard its antiquity or the authority of the men who have maintained it; or we fear the threats it fastens upon unbelievers, or pursue its premises. . . . We are Christians by the same title that we are Perigordians or Germans" (II: 12, 124–25). On the one hand, it appears from this very passage that form or the outer accoutrement, here a religious sect or nationality, is less important than the essence, faith, or inner nature of man. On the other hand, the same passage, when left in the context where it occurs, also decries the accidental nature of the Protestant faith; the two positions, however, are not mutually exclusive. Montaigne can always be detected in a negative stance toward the new Christian sects; of course, this mark of intolerance surprises, since he figures as the model of tolerance and relativism elsewhere. But he consistently expressed himself against the Reformation and its adherents because of its intense disruptive effect upon political and societal life and unity. His fideism then exists as much out of conviction as it does as a shield against those who in his view take extreme positions. This form of fideism can easily be made to reflect a certain conservatism in both religion and politics.[13]

Although the fideistic approach to Montaigne's religious thought prevails among critics, it still leaves some room for other critical opinions. The leading nineteenth-century French critic, Sainte-Beuve, who marks the beginning of modern literary criticism, held to an areligious Montaigne, and at times even an anti-Christian one.[14] A better case could be made for an a-Christian Montaigne than an anti-Christian one. Sainte-Beuve's opinion prevails in Villey's attitude toward Montaigne's religion. Villey, still one of the foremost Montaigne figures during the first third of this century, maintains that the distinctive feature of Montaigne's religion is that it is completely devoid of any religious feeling; reason dominates, and rites are performed almost automatically. Yet this attitude does not deny the fideistic tendencies.[15] Quite logically as a reaction to this critical strain, a Montaigne *bon catholique* would soon appear, proclaimed so by a canon, but rejudged by others as well. Again fideism occupies an important role, but the *Travel Journal* to Italy is used to show instances of Montaigne practicing his faith and exhibiting his piety: eighteen mentions of his going to mass, his taking part in religious processions, his careful account of miracles, of devotions to the Virgin, and of pilgrimages by others.[16] No distinction is made, however, between the believer and the observer; whether and to what extent these religious participations represent acts of piety or an immersion in mores to better grasp and understand the spirit of a people may never be clearly discernible. The crux in deciphering Montaigne's thought lies precisely in attempting to distinguish what he believes from what he says or implies through cascades of examples and experiences.

Two essays, frequently cited in regard to Montaigne's religious thought, "Of Prayers" (I: 56) and "Of Cripples" (III: 11), illustrate the fluidity of this gray zone. In "Of Prayers," Montaigne asserts again in a late addition his good catholicism and implies its accidental nature: "I hold it as execrable if anything is found which was said by me ignorantly or inadvertently, against the holy prescriptions of the Catholic, Apostolic, and Roman Church, in which I die and in which I was born" (p. 229). He attacks the existing superficiality and abuse of prayers: "We pray out of habit and custom, or to speak more correctly, we read or pronounce our prayers. All in all, it is only an act" (pp. 330–31). He declares that even the translation of the Scriptures into French will not diminish the possibilities of interpretations and therefore of confusion. He does not criticize nearly as much the structures of religion as the authenticity of man toward it: "In whatever way we call God to our company and society, it should be seriously and religiously" (p. 234). Montaigne, then, does not reject the essence but the manner. Yet this manner reflects the hypocrisy and the almost inherent evil of civilized man, who must cleanse himself, repent, in order to receive God's pardon, an ideal more than a fact of life: "But still, in return, we must look on her [divine law] in the right way. We must receive this pardon with thanksgiving, and, at least for that instant when we address ourselves to her, have a soul remorseful for its sins and at enmity with the passions that have driven us to offend her" (p. 236). If the success of an individual's religion depends on his willingness to repent, then, by implication, authentic and effective religion fails because Montaigne refuses to repent (cf. "Of Repentance," III: 2), and therefore prayers as performed are useless.

"Of Cripples" deals with miracles and credulity, but its main thesis is the failure of reason and certitude of knowledge. As a rule, we believe what we want to believe, especially if it suits our needs. We have enough to do solving the mysteries of the self without seeking others outside of ourselves; this logic leads to an affirmation of doubting miracles; and of doubt in general: "Let us not look for outside and unknown illusions, we who are perpetually agitated by our own homegrown illusions. It seems to me that we may be pardoned for disbelieving a marvel, at least as long as we can turn aside and avoid the supernatural explanation by nonmarvelous means. And I follow St. Augustine's opinion, that it is better to lean toward doubt than toward assurance in things difficult to prove and dangerous to believe" (pp. 789–90). Yet Montaigne himself, shortly thereafter in the same essay concedes that he, his imagination, falls prey to the "very unreliable appearances given by falsehood" (p. 791). This dichotomy between what reason rejects and what imagination knowingly accepts from false appearance creates a healthy gray zone in religion as well as toward knowledge.[17]

Although a wide consensus exists on Montaigne's fideism, his Christianity continues to elicit widespread questioning in many responsible quarters. Few doubt his religiosity, but most disagree on its label. No matter how religious he may be, some will assert, his religious sentiment is not quite Christian.[18] The point may be well taken that Montaigne reflects the religion of a philosopher whose principle of affirmation is always that of negation; his faith is never totally unshaken nor his wisdom ever constant; he is not a believer without afterthoughts nor an unrestricted freethinker.[19] In the same vein, faith then becomes a superior form of incertitude, an opening unto the empire of transcendental possibilities.[20] So that in the final analysis, only one universal truth exists, the one inside of us which is our very nature, and therein lies Montaigne's deep-seated faith.[21] Yet God does exist, recognizable in our feeling that all is miracle and worthy of veneration. Deism is always a convenient formula out of a religious dilemma, especially in the case of Montaigne's all-embracing and searching mind, at the expense, however, of formal Catholicism or Christianity.

In a discussion of religion in given literary works, distinguishing the author from his work can be most useful. Few will disagree that Montaigne is religious, even Christian, even Catholic, so long as we are talking of the individual. The *Essays*, on the other hand, is the product of his mind, an exploring mind that in the face of new vistas may have led him to entertain anti-Christian ideas. This questioning, in turn, has allowed posterity to impute to Montaigne religious labels that he himself would refute; yet the *Essays* speaks for itself, irrespective of what its author practiced.[22] No wonder, then, the *Essays* was placed on the Index in 1676 and as early as 1640 in Spain. Furthermore, it contains an underlying pagan current that culminates with the prayer to Apollo that ends the *Essays:* "Let us commend it [old age] to that God who is the protector of health and wisdom, but gay and sociable wisdom:

> "Grant me but health, Latona's son,
> And to enjoy the wealth I've won,
> And honored age, with mind entire
> And not unsolaced by the lyre."
>
> Horace (857)

Although this pagan presence is standard in humanistic thought and attests to the syncretism of the Renaissance, the fusion of ancient thought and Christianity, it still dilutes the tenets of a Christian religion.

On an intellectual plane, a struggle of epic proportions between faith and reason occurs in the longest essay of all, the "Apology for Raymond Sebond" (II: 12), numbering about 140 pages in the translated edition used here. As the body of essays appears now, it stands strategically in the middle of the three books and dominates them while casting a significant shadow over the whole corpus. The reader cannot help but ask himself why Montaigne decides to write such a lengthy essay in a prose often rhetorical and different from that of the other essays, even if such a sustained flow does reflect a weighty matter of the author's mind; the "Apology" still stands out for its disproportionate size in relation to the other essays. In addition, because of its rhetorical tone and of a more incisive and articulated style than usual, in which the "I" disappears, this essay figures, in fact, as a sort of an anti-essay, a different sort from the others.

The "Apology" professes the fallibility of reason and the senses. Ostensibly however, as the title indicates, it is written to defend the position taken by a fifteenth-century Spanish philosopher, Raymond Sebond, in his *Natural Theology,* that reason can be used as a tool to substantiate faith. But in fact, Montaigne endeavors to

stress the vanity, the presumption, the insignificance of man—
while still writing the longest and most perplexing essay of them all—
and very soon loses sight of the original impetus and Sebond himself, on the surface at least. A sizable portion of the essay deals with
the shortcomings of knowledge (pp. 358–443), and Montaigne
even claims through an avalanche of examples that animals are
at least as intelligent as man, if not more so in some instances
(pp. 333–58). Montaigne can hardly believe everything he is saying;
exposition dominates over digestion or assimilation, and the
resulting skepticism is as much intellectual acrobatics as conviction.
The articulated conclusion of the essay leaves no doubt: Man's
ignorance leads him to an inevitable submission to God à la Pascal,
but in the meantime Montaigne has written a resounding essay by
the very act of which he shows himself superior to the animals
and exhibits the prowess of his mind.

V   The Human Condition

In a religious framework, the crux of the "Apology" lies in the
traditional conflict between free will and predestination. The
uncertainty of knowledge and the ensuing wretched condition lead
to an inevitable self-abnegation and submission to God's will.
This consciousness makes man dependent on God's grace to
extract him from this earthly morass. Yet man wants to rise above
his condition, above humanity, but can do so only by the grace of
God; this position emerges at the conclusion of the "Apology"
in a post-1588 addition and reworking of the end:

To this most religious conclusion of a pagan [the eternal omnipresence
and omniscience of God] I want to add only this remark of a witness of the
same condition [Seneca], for an ending to this long and boring discourse,
which would give me material without end: "O what a vile and abject
thing is man," he says, "if he does not raise himself above humanity!"
   That is a good statement and a useful desire, but equally absurd. For
to make the handful bigger than the hand, the armful bigger than the arm,
and to hope to straddle more than the reach of our legs, is impossible
and unnatural. Nor can man raise himself above himself and humanity;
for he can see only with his own eyes, and seize only with his own grasp.
   He will rise, if God by exception lends him a hand; he will rise by aban-
doning and renouncing his own means, and letting himself be raised
and uplifted by purely celestial means.

It is for our Christian faith, not for his Stoical virtue, to aspire to that divine and miraculous metamorphosis. (p. 457)

In a religious framework Montaigne may pronounce here a personal dogma to reflect the dominant thesis of this essay, but in the broader framework of the *Essays* as a whole, the rising above humanity remains quite central and even succeeds. As a matter of fact, the very function of the *Essays* is to provide him with a means to rise above humanity. In the course of writing them he gains consciousness of who he is and discovers his universality and at the same time, despite his claims to the contrary, his uniqueness: a creative self-consciousness, his measure of having risen above humanity.

Faith circumvents and refutes knowledge; yet wisdom is awareness of man's place and function in this universe. This consciousness centers about the meaning of life, and in this frame of reference, man's universality: "Each man bears the entire form of man's estate" (III: 2, 611).[23] "Man's estate" here is the translation for *l'humaine condition*, the situation in which man finds himself upon being born. To a modern reader the phrase *l'humaine condition* immediately brings to mind André Malraux's novel *La Condition humaine (Man's Fate)* purporting that action gives meaning to life, mitigates its absurdity, and lets man avoid his fate of simply waiting for death. In "To Philosophize Is to Learn to Die," Montaigne foreshadows this position as he advocates that the soul faces the human condition, death, in order to grow accustomed to it and overcome our fear of it: "For as it is impossible for the soul to be at rest while she fears death, so, if she can gain assurance against it, she can boast of a thing as it were beyond man's estate [*humaine condition*]: that it is impossible for worry, torment, fear, or even the slightest displeasure to dwell in her . . . " (I: 21, 63). If the human condition is death, it behooves man to conquer this predicament. The solution may not lie in faith, but certainly in self-consciousness. For Pascal, Montaigne's successor in the analysis of the human condition and the first one to transpose the phrase in its modern form, *la condition humaine,* man's predicament assumes a relativistic position; man's ability to think counterbalances his insignificance in the universe. Yet Pascal in the final analysis sees a solution only in man's total abnegation before an overwhelming and crushing universe, and in this view faith alone can redeem him.

The concept of the human condition in the *Essays* shifts, but one meaning does not contradict another; each complements the other in order to form a composite and rich whole. The *humaine condition* in "To Philosophize Is to Learn to Die" bears witness to the inevitability of death and how man has to learn to face it and conquer it. This connotation of man's estate remains implicit throughout the *Essays*. A metaphor in the second book adds a new dimension to this generic existential concept as the shift occurs from a metaphysical to an intellectual plane. Montaigne now dwells on his "scar": "So I do not want to forget this further scar, very unfit to produce in public: irresolution, a most harmful failing in negotiating worldly affairs. I do not know which side to take in doubtful enterprises. . ." (II: 17, 496). The mind cannot decide which option to choose in daily living activities or in the more abstract realm of philosophical and ethical thought. Yet this irresolution, no matter how painful it may be, gives the impetus to argumentative thought and writing, to consciousness, and ultimately to cure: "The portrait Montaigne paints in his *Essays* is that of a privatistic man, whose scar is this: ineptitude at taking the lead in most public 'causes,' irresolution in dealing with doubtful enterprise whether they be political, religious, metaphysical, or all three, and the living time in which this scar is embedded in his friendship for his own mental and bodily health."[24]

Man, then, must learn to live with his forced earthly predicament. To begin with, he must insulate himself, but not necessarily isolate himself, from the vicissitudes of life. From this distance he will gain serenity of mind and acceptance of life. To achieve this goal, Montaigne carves out for himself what he calls his "back shop" where he will converse with himself, write his essays, and attempt to be his own master: "We should have wife, children, goods, and above all health, if we can; but we must not bind ourselves to them so strongly that our happiness depends on them. We must reserve a back shop all our own, entirely free, in which to establish our real liberty and our principal retreat and solitude. Here our ordinary conversation must be between us and ourselves, and so private that no private association or communication can find a place; here we must talk and laugh as if without wife, without children, without possessions, without retinue and servants, so that, when the time comes to lose them, it will be nothing new to us to do without them" (I: 39, 177). Montaigne cherishes his independence; yet this distance from others does not preclude a need for others. In fact, the meaning and quality of life depend on a position somewhere between independence and gregariousness. [25] The back shop could not exist without its exterior counterpart and still remain productive. And this independence from others is more an outward appearance than an inner conviction.

The need for others posits its correlative of the relation toward others. The human condition forces an attraction to others after an initial repulsion and even revulsion of others. Montaigne's mixed attitude toward what he terms the vulgar, or the common herd, illustrates his rapport with his fellowman. Being a nobleman, though a recent one, he would exhibit an inherent scorn toward those of a lower social status; [26] yet he directs this same scorn toward those belonging to the nonconscious group, no matter what status they may occupy in life; therefore the moral or the religious is not always clearly distinguishable from the social—perhaps on purpose, in order to dilute personal and unattractive prejudices. He scorns those who cannot think or judge objectively: "For the common herd, not having the faculty of judging things in themselves, let themselves be carried away by chance and by appearances, when once they have been given the temerity to despise and judge the opinions that they held in extreme reverence, such as are those in which their salvation is concerned" (II: 12, 320).

Then this same common herd, previously rejected, is envied in the latter part of the *Essays* for its innate wisdom in the face of the inexorable human condition: "The common people need neither remedy nor consolation except when the blow falls, and consider only precisely as much of it as they feel. Isn't that what we say, that the stupidity and lack of apprehension of the vulgar gives them this endurance of present troubles and this profound nonchalance about sinister accidents to come, that their souls, because they are thick and obtuse, are less penetrable and unstable?" (III: 12, 805). This ambivalence toward the common herd illustrates how Montaigne picks and chooses what fits his thought of the moment; he rejects the vulgar for its thoughtlessness in religion, but praises it for a similar attitude toward death. In either case, he needs others to make his point. No matter how much he relies on his back shop, he still has to communicate with the outside world, be it that of books or people. Here rests the ultimate human condition. Hell may be others, as Sartre declares at the end of *No Exit,* but we must make the best of it—and continue.

In Montaigne's eyes man's estate is to gain a consciousness of his own existence through his intelligence. The essence of life then resides in exercising one's faculty of thinking. This activity in turn reflects a personality that seeks itself, and in the process breaks up because of the contradictions it encounters. What remains of this cerebral distillation is a sense of direction. The road has not been a straight one but a tortuous and circuitous one, but the final destination has been reached through the advocacy of the plenitude of life. Even if in this realization Montaigne projects a low profile for himself, the reader cannot quite take him literally: "I set forth a humble and inglorious life; that does not matter. You can tie up all moral philosophy with a common and private life just as well as with a life of richer stuff" (III: 2, 611). Indeed, Montaigne's life has been much more "of richer stuff" than "common and private." He has resolved the question of how to live, to the fullest, without abdicating any sensual or intellectual privileges, but daily he must still face the human condition, learn from it, and return to his completed essays, constantly adding to them the travails of his mind. Plenitude of life and the descent into himself interlock. Again and again they bring forth indecision and the reality of death, and back to the plenitude of life until the writing freezes this cerebral motion—to be broken by some eventual addition.

VI   *The Universal Malady*

Indeed, the human condition produces a sickness. During the Middle Ages it was called the monks' malady or *acedia,* which Petrarch epitomized; it was a malaise resulting from an inner struggle between the contemplative and the active life. Petrarch never quite overcame it; if he had, he might not have become the seminal humanist that he is. Montaigne, too, suffers from this illness; in one of his early essays, "Of Idleness" (I: 8), he faces a similar spiritual crisis, but the writing of the essays provides a solution to both ends of the dilemma, although he will not admit to it explicitly, and will continue to exonerate himself concerning the endeavor he has undertaken. However, soon after starting the composition of the *Essays,* he will begin to suffer from a physiological illness that will absorb him and assume metaphorical dimensions for his existential being.

In 1578 Montaigne had his first attacks of kidney stones. All his adult life to that time he had feared this because his father had suffered and died of the same illness. The fear of pain in the early essays is due in part to his apprehension and premonition of this sickness. In one of the first essays, "That the Taste of Good and Evil Depends in Large Part on the Opinion We Have of Them" (I: 14), he attempts to overcome this fear by stressing his contempt for it and by pointing out that it is more a state of mind than a physical condition, and man has to learn to control both, a view substantiated even by the post-1588 additions: "It is easy to see that what makes pain and pleasure keen in us is the sharpness of our mind . . . . Each man is as well or as badly off as he thinks he is. Not the man of whom it is thought, but the one who thinks it of himself, is happy. And by just this fact belief gains reality and truth . . . . *The whole thing is to be master of yourself* [Cicero]" (pp. 39, 46, 47).

However, when the illness strikes, a shift occurs from the abstract to a concrete lived experience. Yet Montaigne makes the best of it and profits from it immeasurably. To begin with, his stones free him from the fear of suffering and death because they give his anxieties an immediacy that forces him to cope with them readily. At this point the physiological, supplanting the metaphysical, reinforces philosophy, or still better, it becomes its metaphor. His stones, just like philosophy, teach him how to live and how to die. His illness, however, holds a significant advantage over philosophy; the latter remains an abstraction emanating from others and acting upon him, but the stones provide the personal experience from within himself. In this sense, this sickness is the midpoint metaphor in the curve that buttresses the *Essays*—from exteriorization to interiorization of reflexion—and it is no structural accident that the first full account of his kidney ailment occurs in the last essay of the second book, "Of the Resemblance of Children to Fathers," because the third book marks this interiorization:

I am at grips with the worst of all maladies, the most sudden, the most painful, the most mortal, and the most irremediable. I have already experienced five or six very long and painful bouts of it. However, either I flatter myself or else there is even in this condition enough to bear up a man whose soul is unburdened of the fear of death and unburdened of the threats, sentences, and consequences which medicine dins into our ears. But the very impact of the pain has not such sharp and piercing bitterness as to drive a well-poised man to madness or despair. I have at least this profit from the stone, that it will complete what I have still not been able to accomplish in myself and reconcile and familiarize me completely with death: for the more my illness oppresses and bothers me, the less will death be something for me to fear. (II: 37, 576)

Montaigne grows accustomed to his "colicky life" (p. 575); indeed he ends up welcoming it, because it becomes the very source of his spiritual health. Repeatedly he takes a stand against medicine and doctors because they are either human or haphazard, and therefore, ineffective, and he holds to this position to the very end: "The art of medicine is not so fixed that we are without authority, no matter what we do; it changes according to the climates and according to the moons, according to Fernel and according to L'Escale. If your doctor does not think it good for you to sleep, to drink wine, or to eat such-and-such a food, don't worry: I'll find you another who will not agree with him. The variety of medical arguments and opinions embraces all kinds of forms" (III: 13, 833). In the face of a gradually decaying body and an increasingly gripping sickness, Montaigne does not flinch; he alters his style of living as little as possible. Instead of depending on medical science, he prefers to let nature take its course or use natural means of cure; in this view he prefigures Molière. One partial reason for his trip to Italy in 1580–81 was to visit spas there and drink their water that would supposedly help his stones; the real aim of this voyage, however, was to assuage his wanderlust and to engage in a concrete exploration of new lands, concrete and intellectual, that would later contribute to his *Essays*.

In the final analysis, Montaigne believes he himself is his own best doctor: "In the end I recognized that the surest thing was to entrust myself and my need to myself" (III: 12, 799). This conviction of Montaigne is not due solely to his mistrust of the medical profession, outside knowledge, but as well to his desire to remain free to exercise various options and maintain his self-mastery: "True freedom is to have power over oneself for everything" (p. 800). Montaigne did not always enjoy this position of freedom and self-mastery, but it was always an ideal, and at the end of the *Essays* it becomes a reality, because he attains self-knowledge to the extent that it is possible to do so. And his sickness contributes vastly toward his reaching this position of consciousness. Physiologically his stones cause acute suffering, and in his mind this pain makes him all the more aware of the human condition, of death, and through this immediacy helps him to overcome it. As a matter of fact, this sickness holds such a tight grip over him because it reflects a dominant state of mind: a constant attempt to come to terms with something threatening or obsessive. Ultimately, then, the sickness becomes the source of the cure, and the stones are therefore transformed into an object of praise. In fact, Montaigne enjoys his sickness, knowing full well that as a result of it health cannot be far around the corner; to live therefore means to oscillate between health and illness, although the perfect condition would be a constant midway point. However, in practice Montaigne prefers paradoxically a state of sickness, of painful consciousness, because he can then look forward to health and serenity; on the other hand, when in health only another attack of kidney stones awaits him.

VII   *Commitment: Limited and Full*

A principal source of spiritual illness and existential crisis lies in the question of commitment. In this instance the oscillation occurs for a while between public and private life. Montaigne's course of action soon favors the latter, though this decision, which he will not regret, never quite gives him peace of mind. The image of a Montaigne who retires to the ivory tower of his library, first in 1571 and then in 1585, away from the glaring and critical public eye, should also allow for a Montaigne who has to reconcile these decisions with himself, with his contemporaries, and with his readers.

When Montaigne in 1571 resigned as councillor to the parliament of Bordeaux to dedicate himself to the "bosom of the learned virgins," he felt that he could make better use of his time cultivating his mind and writing than facing the daily frustrations of indecision in political matters and distasteful decisions in public life. Any guilt resulting from this resignation stayed within himself, that is, between his private self and the one still committed to public involvement. However, he never believed that he had made the wrong decision, and from 1571 to 1585 any self-apology was addressed more to himself than to others. In his view, action in the outside world had to take place within fixed guidelines, with little room for flexibility and imagination, whereas the life of thought and creativity gave him freedom of action and movement. Private life never loses its superiority over the public life. The almost unchallenged hegemony of private life then dominates the first two books, and this position is summed up and best seen in the essay "Of Custom, and Not Easily Changing an Accepted Law": "the wise man should withdraw his soul within, out of the crowd, and keep it in freedom and power to judge things freely; but as for externals, he should wholly follow the accepted fashions and forms. Society in general can do without our thoughts; but the rest—our actions, our work, our fortunes, and our very life—we must lend and abandon to its service and to the common opinions. For it is the rule of rules, and the universal of laws, that each man should observe those of the place he is in" (I: 23, 86). Montaigne advocates, therefore, a detached and independent inner being while the outer being, the one known and judged by others, conforms as much as possible to the norms and laws of society. Thus, within himself he achieves flexibility.

However, society exerts overwhelming pressure on an individual, especially if he attempts to achieve a balance between detachment and limited or apparent involvement. Montaigne believes that one should not shirk public involvement and civic obligations, but one should not give himself totally to these endeavors. In this spirit, Montaigne accepted the mayoralty of Bordeaux in 1581 at the urging of the king, Henry III, interrupted his stay in Italy, and returned to assume his duties. He served two two-year terms, refused to serve any more, and refused to return to Bordeaux from his home and help with the inauguration of his successor; these two refusals were due in great part to his fear of the plague which raged in the city. If he did not quite behave like Camus's Dr. Rieux in *The Plague*, who stayed in the press though completely aware of his eventual failure, he always felt he had made the right decisions. But evidently his contemporaries did not think so, because one of the main thrusts of the third book of essays is Montaigne's explanation of what involvement means to him; the commitment to his *Essays* supersedes that to society and may even be more beneficial to it.[27]

Of utmost importance in this vein is the fact that the first essay of the third book, "Of the Useful and the Honorable," deals squarely and fully with the question of an individual's commitment to society, law, and the king. Its initial position is no mere accident, and the contrast it offers with the first essays in the first two books points to the obsessive nature of this question. "By Diverse Means We Arrive at the Same End" (I: 1) and "Of the Inconsistency of Our Actions" (II: 1), as suggested by their very titles, stress the multiplicity of truth and human behavior and thereby act as thematic antechambers to the essays they precede. In this regard, the second essay of the third book, "Of Repentance," would continue the thematic and structural pattern of the first essays in the first two books because here again Montaigne advocates diversity of thought and action by maintaining the validity of what he has said and done in the past or will say or do in the future despite any apparent contradictions that may arise. "Of Repentance," then, would be the logical beginning of his renewed efforts that were to come to fruit in 1588. But "Of the Useful and the Honorable," despite its apparently disruptive position, has precedence in order to allow for a special self-apology that was to continue to reverberate strongly throughout the third book, since Montaigne needs to defend his deeds of 1585. Such a conjecture may not be an idle one.

Montaigne argues that the nature of involvement and usefulness of an action remain a relative matter to be judged on an individualistic basis; in this light, of course, his retirement from public life, the events of 1585, and his act of writing the essays become ambivalent and positive respectively. As a result, the line of demarcation between the good and the bad of the private and common interest is blurred and so is the differentiation between the private and the common interest:

Let us not fear . . . to consider . . . that the common interest must not require all things of all men against the private interest . . . and that not all things are permissible for an honorable man in the service of his king, or of the common cause, or of the laws . . . . It is a lesson proper for the times. We have no need to harden our hearts with these plates of steel, it is enough to harden our shoulders; it is enough to dip our pens in ink without dipping them in blood.

We poorly argue the honor and beauty of an action from its utility, and we commit a fallacy in thinking that everyone is obliged to perform— and that it is honorable for everyone to perform—an action merely because it is useful . . . (III: 1, pp. 609, 610)

And Montaigne ends the essay by asserting that although marriage is a most universal foundation of society, those in the "most venerable vocation of men," the priests, are excluded from it (p. 610). Is marriage good or bad then? The final statement tilts the balance toward a positive attitude: "as we assign to stud those horses [i.e., priests] which are of least value" (p. 610). Montaigne

may seek to disconcert the reader, but above all he observes from
a distance with a sly, superior, and uncommitted smile.

This ambivalence announces the crucial point that no involvement should be so total as not to permit disengagement at any
time. Montaigne makes this position clear in one of his last essays,
"Of Husbanding Your Will" (III:10). Moreover, he distinguishes
clearly in this context between a chameleon-like outer self and a
constant inner self threatened by any overcommitment:

> The mayor and Montaigne have always been two, with a very clear separa-
> tion. For all of being a lawyer or a financier, we must not ignore the knavery
> there is in such callings. As honest man is not accountable for the vice
> or stupidity of his trade, and should not therefore refuse to practice it:
> it is the custom of his country, and there is profit in it. We must live in the
> world and make the most of it such as we find it.
>
> I do not know how to involve myself so deeply and so entirely. When
> my will gives me over to one party it is not so violent an obligation that
> my understanding is infected by it . . . . People adore everything that is
> on their side; as for me, I do not even excuse most of the things that I see
> on mine. A good work does not lose its grace for pleading against my cause.
> (p. 774)

Commitment occurs, therefore, much more with the body than
with the soul. This distance allows for dispassionateness and
objectivity. Montaigne participates in an exterior life—involvement,
by force of habit, prudence, and necessity, inasmuch as it will
contribute to the formation of his inner self because he aims at
obtaining a harmony of the interior self by means of an equilibrium
between extremes. Thus conscience and self-consciousness dictate
a dispassionate public commitment.

The private involvement is with the self and in turn with the
writing of the *Essays* that reflects this self. In other words, the
chain of reflection begins with public commitment, affects the
inner self and ends up in the *Essays*. However, a more direct relation exists between public involvement and the essays, for the content
and form of the latter reflect the nature of the public commitment.
Just as Montaigne gives of himself only partially to causes and
parties in order to conserve his autonomy, so he does in the essays,
where he never takes an irrevocable stance. The skepticism and
stoicism that pervade the *Essays* find their counterpart in a dispassionate and dubious involvement in public life; the nature of
intellectual, political, and social commitment follows that same

particular bent of disengagement. And paradoxically, Montaigne's own brand of solitude, retirement from private life, is transformed into a supreme form of commitment through the actuation of the *Essays*.[28]

VIII *Society, Laws, and Customs*

The dilemma of commitment, involvement in public life and society, brings into focus a moral morass and raises a fundamental existential question. Under what precepts, customs, or laws should man function in society? The answer would be easy if Montaigne differentiated clearly between good and evil, but as a rule the line of demarcation between vice and virtue remains blurred except when obvious extremes enter in play. He takes, for example, a definite stand against cruelty, not only in his essay "Of Cruelty" (II: 11), but throughout the *Essays*. He leaves little doubt about his adverse feelings toward witchcraft in "Of Cripples" (III: 11), and toward judicial torture in "Of Conscience" (II: 5). Conscience itself and reason, despite its limitations, dictate of course such humane attitudes. Most of the time he does not tolerate hypocrisy, and in "On Some Verses of Virgil" (III: 5) he states flatly that a spade ought to be called a spade, there is no need of periphrase or euphemisms to express physiological or sexual acts.

Although in the final analysis Montaigne favors customs over laws, some fluidity still comes to the fore in regard to these two matters. Customs attract him because they bear out the concept of diversity so fundamental to his thought, and they provide therefore intellectual options and critical freedom. They also give him a sense of individuality and distance between him and the ancients, since customs vary in time and space. Above all, they break down the barrier between right and wrong, between good and evil, and thereby shift attention to mores rather than morality. Montaigne is more interested in the types of life men lead or have led and in the various means of being that men choose for themselves rather than in the morality of their actions. Customs, then, appeal to his sense and need of mobilism and provide a flexible foundation to learning how to cope with one's existence and inserting and disengaging oneself from society, for their very diversity lends itself to casuistic possibilities.

On the other hand, laws are rigid and arbitrary, despite their boundless number. In fact, their very multiplicity reflects their limit, since new laws are constantly enacted to fit or circumvent a given situation or case; there will never be enough laws to satisfy varied and everchanging human actions; hence the laws of nature or customs receive Montaigne's blessing at this juncture: "There is little relation between our actions, which are in perpetual mutation, and fixed and immutable laws. The most desirable are those that are rarest, simplest, and most general, and I even think it would be better to have none at all than to have them in such numbers as we have. Nature always gives us happier laws than those we give ourselves" (III: 13, 816). Moreover, intrinsically laws contain no equitable basis, above all because they are man-made, yet upon their enactment they have an almost frightening and inexplicable authoritative power that indicates an unfortunate if not tragic disproportion between the laws and their fallible makers: "Now laws remain in credit not because they are just, but because they are laws. That is the mystic foundation of their authority; they have no other. And that is a good thing for them. They are often made by fools, more often by people, who in their hatred of equality, are wanting in equity; but always by men, vain and irresolute authors. There is nothing so grossly and widely and ordinarily faulty as the laws. Whoever obeys them because they are just, does not obey them for just the reason he should" (p. 821). Although such a statement smacks somewhat of anarchical and even revolutionary sentiments, it is elicited by a sense of justice, not along class lines but based on reason and good judgment and even against an unattainable absolute. However, man still lives in a rather rotten society and has to make the best of it.

Montaigne leans toward the status quo much more by necessity than by choice. He would not advocate rapid and abrupt change but a slow, progressive one. His opting for the existing form of government in France does not mean that he favors political absolutism, but rather that he is willing to live with a working system and avoid the unknown of change: "Nothing presses a state hard except innovation; change alone lends shape to injustice and tyranny. When some part is dislocated, we can prop it up; we can fight against letting the alteration and corruption natural to all things carry us too far from our beginnings and principles. But to undertake to recast so great a mass, to change the foundations of so great a structure, that is a job for those who wipe out a picture in order to clean it, who want to reform defects of detail by universal confusion and cure illnesses by death" (III: 9, 731). Faced with disorder and instability about him, man seeks order and stability; thus mutability leads to measure and balance. And custom returns to the fore: "Not in theory, but in truth, the best and most excellent government for each nation is the one under which it has preserved its existence. Its form and essential fitness depend on habit. We are prone to be discontented with the present state of things. But I maintain, nevertheless, that to wish for the government of a few in a democratic state, or another type of government in a monarchy, is foolish and wrong" (*ibid.*). Law, especially common law, and custom become one then and interchangeable.[29] The human condition in this instance is reduced to a search for permanence, eventually achieved within the inner self but always questioned and critically scrutinized as it applies to the outside world.

Stability results from close scrutiny of accepted norms and self-scrutiny, and from a constant process of reevaluation; hence stability produces flexibility and relativism. Thus, on the ethical plane, the *Essays* propounds a variable morality, at times even egotistical and tailor-made to fit given individuals. In fact, Montaigne's moral stance comes about as much from experience as from the critical examination taking place within the essay itself. Of course, Montaigne sharply condemns vice and views it as deriving from ignorance: "There is no vice truly a vice which is not offensive, and which a sound judgment does not condemn; for its ugliness and painfulness are so apparent that perhaps the people are right who say it is chiefly produced by stupidity and ignorance. So hard it is to imagine anyone knowing it without hating it" (III: 2, 612). Yet in the very same essay he suggests that a vice does not exist intrinsically, but in the mind of others, unless the individual himself is convinced of it. Therefore the individual remains the ultimate judge, and this position dilutes and diminishes the frequency and strength of the vice.[30] In addition, as usual, Montaigne shifts from an absolute to a more fluid attitude. Essentially, then, vice, just like commitment, remains a question of judgment and not a thought or action projected against some arbitrary standard: "There is no one but yourself who knows whether you are cowardly and cruel, or loyal and devout. Others do not see you, they guess at you by uncertain conjectures; they see not so much your nature as your art. Therefore do not cling to their judgment; cling to your own" (p. 613).

IX *Education and the World Stage*

To this end of self-judgment, education enters the picture, because for Montaigne education does not constitute a means of acquiring factual knowledge (a dubious achievement in his eyes), but of forming one's ability to judge along lines that will benefit one's intellect and conduct. Montaigne expresses his pedagogical views in two successive essays, "Of Pedantry" (I: 25) and "Of the Education of Children" (I: 26), but principally in the latter. A traditional exercise is to compare Montaigne's pedagogical views with those of Rabelais, his humanistic predecessor. This standard confrontation between the two dominant figures of the century leads to the somewhat erroneous conclusion that the author of *Gargantua and Pantagruel* advocates a well-filled head, an accumulation of as much knowledge as possible; on the other hand, the author of the *Essays* believes in a well-formed head, that is, the assimilation of selected and functional material that will forge a critical thinker and well-behaved gentleman, the forerunner of the seventeenth-century *honnête homme* or perfect gentleman. But Rabelais may stuff his giants with an inordinate amount of learning and wish that they become an "abyss of knowledge," a more direct result of their size than his own indiscriminate conviction, yet it is too often forgotten that in his *Tiers Livre* (Third Book) he comes to the conclusion that certain knowledge is impossible and vain, and only within ourselves can we know anything with any valid certainty at all, since we can only be assured of knowing just ourselves—a position akin to Montaigne's and rather typical of the Renaissance humanist. [31]

Education, in Montaigne's essays, has a critical and dynamic function rather than a theoretical one. To begin with, it will provide self-awareness: "Let him know that he knows, at least" (I: 26, 111). The student must remain flexible and available, and he will become involved only in causes he approves (p. 114). He will deal with histories, not to learn them, but to judge them. Learning to cope with pain becomes an integral part of education. In keeping with the humanistic tradition, body and mind receive equal attention in the pedagogical framework of a child. Methodologically Montaigne advocates a mixture of gentleness and force, a "severe gentleness" (p. 122); he does so by alluding to two of Ariosto's heroines in *Orlando furioso*, Bradamante, the female warrior, and Angelica, the Eternal Feminine (p. 119).

Because "the world is nothing but babble" (p. 124), words gain the supremacy over human beings, and therefore education loses its humanity and practicality. But learning derives its worth from translating words into action; the abstract finds a concrete outlet in order to justify its validity: "He will not so much say his lesson as do it. He will repeat it in his actions . . . . The true mirror of our discourse is the course of our lives" (p. 124). Herein lies a fundamental difference between the pedant and the learned man. Rousseau later, in his *Emile*, will also stress the utility and practicality of education, although his examples are not always felicitous. Because travel exposes one widely to the human endeavor, it affords a preferred means for forming the judgment. Experience does not supplant the book; on the contrary, the two have to mesh together to bring about an educated person (see "Of Books", II: 10, and "Of Three Kinds of Association", III: 3). If the goal of education remains rather monolithic—the formation of a critical judgment— its concept stands out through its multifariousness: "The bees plunder the flowers here and there, but afterward they make of them honey, which is all theirs; it is no longer thyme or marjoram. Even so with the pieces borrowed from others; he will transform and blend them to make a work that is all his own, to wit, his judgment. His education, work, and study aim only at forming this" (p. 111).

Montaigne may be expounding his views on education, but in the process he ultimately draws a self-portrait. He advocates the type of mind that he himself has, a roaming intellect that picks here and there and then creates his own product, the *Essays*. To this double end of education and didactic creativity, he encourages and indulges in what he terms a "commerce," an intellectual exchange, with books and men, that operates on a process of "incessantly filling up and pouring out" (p. 107). What he garners from others educates him; it becomes the substance, then, of his *Essays*, which will hopefully educate others. The dynamics of learning, civilization, and progress lie in this cyclical and to-and-fro flow.

If learning and judgment form man, they do so not by being a mere adornment, but an integral part of him that assumes complete assimilation. Indeed, education aims to strip the adornment and mask and to induce the real self through assimilation of learning. In "Of the Education of Children" (I: 26), frequency of a metaphoric alimentary and digestive language attests to and stresses the fundamental notion of the assimilation of learning and knowledge;[32] hence education becomes part of the person, both in his spirit and in his actions. However, if this essay and the preceding one, "Of Pedantry," are considered as one whole, there emerges a bold and distinct theatrical vocabulary, and an interest in the theater which take on a metaphorical meaning.

Pedantry is a concern with the exterior, with appearances, empty gesticulations, words—the mask—instead of with the interior, with essence, the self-aware being, authentic deeds. In fact, the pedant as a comic theater figure is born during the Renaissance, more precisely at the beginning of the sixteenth century via the Italian stage. The antimedieval and scholastic role assigned to the pedant in comedy acquires the metaphoric meaning of existential inauthenticity in the *Essays*. Montaigne considers the pedant an unconscious, narrow-minded, mechanical being, misusing his knowledge and warped by it: "Whoever will closely observe this sort of people, who are very widespread, will find, as I have, that most of the time they understand neither themselves nor others, and that they have a full enough memory but an entirely hollow judgment . . ." (I: 25, 102). The pedant wears the mask of knowledge but does not understand; his actions and his words do not reflect his thoughts or lack of thoughts;[33] he plays a role but hides his real being; he is true neither to others nor to himself; therefore, "What is the use of learning, if understanding is absent?" (p. 103).

Yet theater can contribute to understanding; that is why Montaigne devotes the last two pages of the essay on education to a praise of the virtues of the stage. He recalls that he himself enjoyed reading classical and Italian comedies and acted in several Latin tragedies. And he concludes by advocating a more enlightened policy on the part of those who rule toward actors and the theater:

For I have always blamed as undiscerning those who condemn these recreations, and as unjust those who refuse entry into our good towns to the comedians who deserve it, and begrudge the people these public amusements. Good governments take care to assemble the citizens and bring them together for sports and amusements as well as for the serious functions of piety; sociability and friendliness are thereby increased. And besides, they could not be granted more orderly pastimes than those that take place in the presence of everyone and right in the sight of the magistrate. And I should think it reasonable that the magistrate and the prince, at their own expense, should sometimes give the people their treat, out of a sort of paternal goodness and affection; and that in populous cities there should be places intended and arranged for these spectacles—a diversion from worse and hidden doings. (I: 26, 131)

Despite Montaigne's admonitions, actors were to remain second-class citizens at least through the eighteenth century and to be denied burial in Christian cemeteries.

Although basing his present arguments on the grounds of bene-volent paternalism and "piety," he had previously stated in the same essay the more profound reasons why men should participate in spectacles, namely, to "be spectators of the life of other men in order to judge and regulate their own" (p. 117). Theater and actors, then, become a metaphor; they provide a means to judge and be judged through physical or spiritual involvement. Montaigne, spectator of his readings and his contemporaries, and we the readers, spectators of his *Essays,* are to be educated from these respective activities. Education, then, enables us to distinguish the phony actor, the pedant, from the genuine one, the discriminating and receptive man. Furthermore, spectator-actors cannot borrow, must assimilate, in order to gain the essential and not appearances, in order to know themselves and be known by others: "Strength and sinews are not to be borrowed; the attire and the cloak may be borrowed" (pp. 127–28). Being on the stage, a metaphor for reading and writing, the actor exposes himself, and he must do so genuinely to be of utmost import and usefulness.[34]

X *Communicating*

To expound a philosophy of education, itself a reflection of the self, is a means of communicating with others, of attempting to communicate this self to others and seeking others out. "Of Friend-ship" embodies this need. In this essay Montaigne not only eulogizes his dead friend Etienne de La Boétie, but their unique friendship as well, unique because each was instinctively attracted to the other and spiritually fused with the other in a "sacred bond . . . because it was he, because it was I" (I : 28, 138, 139).[35] This relationship afforded Montaigne the opportunity to relate unhindered to a fellow human being. Unfortunately, or perhaps fortunately, this friendship lasted only four years; La Boétie died in 1563. The arrest of communication occasioned a very long letter from Montaigne to his father describing his friend's death and becoming in essence a pre-essay (pp. 1046–56); above all, it provided the impetus to Montaigne's eventually turning to the writing of essays to substitute for this loss.[36]

"Of Friendship" is an epitaph to a friend and a friendship that

Montaigne never attained again with another fellow human being. On the other hand, however, although Montaigne suffers intensely from this loss and claims that his life is "nothing but smoke, nothing but dark and dreary night" (p. 143), the friendship in retrospect remains somewhat idealized. The long separation from La Boétie— at least ten years elapsed between his death and the writing of the essay—intensified and crystallized the friendship in Montaigne's mind long after he actually lived it; such a psychological process occurs naturally. Furthermore, as he often does, Montaigne has inverted commonly accepted meanings of words; what he calls friendship we would refer to as love, and love, especially conjugal love, becomes in his eyes what we would accept as friendship. Montaigne also set out in this essay to rehabilitate his friend's political work, *Voluntary Servitude;* instead, he indulged in an argumentative discussion of a humanistic topic, friendship, in the tradition of Cicero, reversing accepted concepts and offering a Platonic, idealistic portrait of uniqueness. This discussion, however, soon loses sight of his friend's literary contribution and suggests in the final analysis the perfection and uniqueness of his own essay. He does present La Boétie's rather dry twenty-nine sonnets in the following essay, but posterity remembers his very own essay, the monument to this friendship, and not La Boétie himself. The lived experience gives way to the literary experience. The dialogue between Montaigne and La Boétie, prematurely interrupted, continues in the writing of the *Essays* between Montaigne and himself and between Montaigne and his readers.

An intriguing conjecture, an idle one like most, is what kind of work, if any, would Montaigne have written if fate had given his relation with La Boétie an opportunity to endure longer. One can assume safely that had this friendship persisted, some written work by Montaigne still would have emerged, because years later toward the end of his life, despite his close spiritual relationship with Mlle de Gournay, his eventual first editor, he still continued to add to his essays. His ultimate friends are his *Essays*.

Friendship is a euphemism for communication and the need thereof. Communication occurs through dialogue—writing or conversing, and through the transmission of signs. Although the *Essays* as a whole conveys a massive and successful effort at communication, some specific ones are devoted to the question.[37] On occasion some admirable short essays focus on means of communications that come to rest metaphorically on how and why Montaigne writes. "Of Riding Post" (II: 22), only slightly more than a page long, was even less than half that before additions were made. Here Montaigne enumerates various ways of sending news: with horsemen who change mount on the way, with birds or pigeons, and with men who ride on other men. The last example he gives (a last addition), marking the end of the essay, deserves particular attention, since it reflects metaphorically his own way of thinking and writing, of gathering ideas and examples from this writer or that source, and his commitment to endure and make the best of the human condition: "I understand that the Wallachians, couriers of the Great Sultan, make extraordinary speed, because they have the right to dismount the first passerby they meet on their way, giving him their jaded horse; and that to guard against tiring, they bind themselves very tightly around the waist with a broad band" (p. 516).

Signs raise the question of the multiplicity of meaning and its transmission. The object used matters less than its potential suggestive power and its vicissitudes through time and space; in fact, its apparent strangeness draws all the more attention. "Of Thumbs" (II: 26), barely a page long, illustrates this part of the human anatomy as a sign, both metaphoric and visual, of a bond between two men (interlocking two bloody thumbs), of favor or disfavor in Rome depending on whether it points upward or downward, of eligibility for military service and capacity for combat, and finally (the last example seemingly playful and gratuitous): "In Lacedaemon the schoolmaster chastised children by biting their thumbs" (p. 523). The thumb, then, communicates the notions of power and vulnerability to pride and above all to human dignity, especially in the last example. Significantly enough, in this instance the shortness of the essay conveys the obliqueness of the sign, and by virtue of this very brevity the essay itself is transformed into a sign.

In a later essay, a long and developed one, bearing the same title (III: 6), coaches become the sign of communication and commitment on a spatial and temporal level, a means to move from one place to another, to participate in combat, and metaphorically to transmit the concepts of wealth and progress through the centuries. Moreover, thumbs and coaches seen as signs allow a given man on a literal and figurative level to stand above others and at the same time run the danger of falling off or being knocked down (cf. especially the end of "Of Coaches," p. 699). Montaigne wants to learn about new spaces and their history; hence the importance of the metaphoric voyage, but in the process, this need of discovering and communicating is fraught with danger of self-injury or self-destruction; he leaves no doubt, however, that the risk is well worth taking.

As a rule, dialogue constitutes the best means of communication because it produces an exchange of points of view, in Montaigne's case between him and his readings and/or experiences and between him and his readers. In fact, he considers this question of conversation so important that he devotes one of his last essays to this topic, "Of the Art of Discussion" (III: 8), and comes to the conclusion that the real winner of an argument is the one who has learned from the discussion and learned how to discuss; hence the function of the *Essays.* The fluidity of truth causes this uncertainty of judgment but assuredness of methodology:

. . . in arguments and discussions not all the remarks that seem good to us should be accepted immediately. Most men are rich with borrowed capacity. It may happen to a given man to make a fine point, a good answer and maxim, and put it forward without recognizing its force. That we do not possess all we borrow may perhaps be verified in myself. We must not always yield to it, whatever truth or beauty it may have. We must either deliberately oppose it, or draw back under color of not understanding it, in order to feel out on all sides how it is lodged in its author. It may happen that we run on the point of his sword and help his blow to carry beyond his reach. (III: 8, 715)

Again Montaigne stands at midpoint between how he reads others and how we should read him. And he does not fear contradictions; indeed, he seeks them out, for they "merely arouse and exercise" him (p. 705). He suggests, therefore, that the discussion, the mode of the essay, pleases more the intellect and resists more the vagaries of imagination than the brittle truth. By asserting the value and effectiveness of discussion, of communication, of writing the *Essays,* Montaigne indicates a certain hegemony of art over truth, very much in a Proustian or Pirandellian vein.

The search for the self and its relationship to the human condition produce the *Essays.* In the face of contradictions toward which it leans simultaneously, the self assimilates them all and settles upon a natural bent to accept life and itself as they have become after a series of bookish and experiential encounters. The human condition upon which death towers remains constant, whereas the self shifts its attitudes toward it and finally there comes the realization that plenitude of life matters above all. Yet this acceptance of the self and this commitment to life do not eliminate the shrinkage of time that hopefully should be overcome in the ultimate victory over the human condition. Hence the sublime commitment to communicate to others the vicissitudes of the self, potentially of Everyman, to write the *Essays,* an act that momentarily freezes the mutability of the self. Montaigne reduces all experiential participation to the function of the self, and this existential centralization escapes mere egotism and acquirès a sublimated life if it conquers time, if it is transmuted into a timeless form, into the word. Man and word become one; Montaigne achieves consubstantiality.

CHAPTER 4

From the Limits of Knowledge to Words Time and Images

MONTAIGNE'S basic assumption is the Socratic precept that to know that one does not know is already to know; seen in this light, knowledge and ignorance become synonymous. Of course, such a realization occurs only after a lengthy and profitable spiritual journey which puts into question human judgment, reason, intelligence, and language. In the meantime, vanity urges man to assume knowledge while fate destroys it or makes its validity inexplicable. Time, then, becomes a creative factor that redeems this state of positive ignorance, and the invention of a personalized metaphoric language contributes further toward overcoming the inconsistencies of knowledge. In fact, Montaigne's critique of knowledge does not aim at eliminating any form of it, but rather at shifting its focus from the inpenetrable metaphysical to the more palpable self. Inevitably, however, any form of knowledge reveals a discrepancy between thought and its object, and from this abyss, and in an attempt to bridge it, is born the essay. In the final analysis, the essential critical task is to try to discern how much Montaigne really does not know and how much he feigns not knowing. This game produces a mystifying inscrutability that comes to rest on an introspection and on the certitude of the validity of the journey.

I *From Ignorance to Knowledge*

Ignorance reflects a state of wonderment or of total helplessness until it is transformed into a self-awareness and a positive if not ultimate source of knowing. To pretend to knowledge may be the most extreme and absurd manifestation of human vanity, yet without curiosity a thinking man is dead and so is the *Essays*. Montaigne asks the question, ascertains the fact, but remains baffled and wonderstruck—for instance, by the process of human procreation, because it exemplifies the limits of human inquiry, the dominance of ignorance: "What a prodigy it is that the drop of seed from which we are produced bears in itself the impressions not only of the bodily form but of the thoughts and inclinations of our fathers! Where does that drop of fluid lodge this infinite number of forms? And how do they convey these resemblances with so heedless and irregular a course that the great-grandson will correspond to his greatgrandfather, the nephew to the uncle?" (II: 37, 578). This statement suggests the miracle of physiological as well as intellectual and artistic procreation, the very composition and mode of the *Essays*. Not only does nature reflect an infinite richness, but it manifests an incomprehensible order that challenges judgment and reason. The mind submits numbly and integrates itself with a checkmate situation, though not before it has questioned and marveled at this phenomenon. Indeed, what stymies the mind every time is the phenomenon, the outer appearances, which keep it from reaching the essence. This frustration pervades the thinking process.

As a result, the mind wallows in inconsistency and mutability. Of course, this state exists only as long as reason and judgment attempt to cope with phenomena, and it lessens somewhat when intelligence turns inward toward the self. Although Montaigne despairs at times, this awareness of flux still has a salutary function in that it triggers curiosity: "Finally, there is no existence that is constant, either of our being or that of objects. And we, and our judgment, and all mortal things go on flowing and rolling unceasingly. Thus nothing certain can be established about one thing by another, both the judging and the judged being in continual change and motion" (II: 12, 455). This claim to ignorance may be genuine, yet on the other hand it provides the impulse for thinking and writing instead of leaving Montaigne in a state of intellectual and creative sterility. In the throes of ignorance, or supposed ignorance, he moves back and forth from an awareness of the inconsistency about him, producing an intellectual movement, to an incessant tendency toward moderation and ataraxy.

Ultimately, in the last book, Montaigne comes to the explicit realization that ignorance is knowledge. To begin with, to discourse of nothing is already to discourse of something; but this verbal and intellectual game veils the fact that the supposed nothing is actually something quite valuable. The sifting process in critically examining all possible facets of a question may lead to a suspended judgment; however, this result cannot be labeled ignorance. On the contrary, the residual product, no matter how small, is knowledge and stands as a most convincing monument against vanity in the *Essays*. In fact, the purported deprecation of this epistemological process reveals instead the very wisdom of it: "I speak ignorance pompously and opulently, and speak knowledge meagerly and piteously, the latter secondarily and accidentally, the former expressly and principally. And there is nothing I treat specifically except nothing, and no knowledge except that of the lack of knowledge" (III: 12, 809).[1] Montaigne arrives at this position after lengthy peregrinations during which judgment has been tested and perfected and experience accumulated. This impossibility of knowledge leads him to turn to within himself; even here, though, satisfactory knowledge remains elusive because to assume it is in itself an admission of ignorance.[2] To claim ignorance and believe in it implies its praise; yet in the final analysis, to Montaigne this praise is meant for a quintessential knowledge, distilled Socratic wisdom, the convergence of little and much knowing: "It is from my experience that I affirm ignorance, which is, in my opinion, the most certain fact in the school of the world" (III: 13, 824).[3]

II   *Vanity and Fortune*

A presumption to knowledge is vanity. Inconsistency and mutability drown out this vanity in such an essay as the "Apology for Raymond Sebond" (II: 12), but also modulate it. To begin with, Montaigne has no illusion of perfection; the ultimate goal is a constantly moving point within a reachable but unsatisfying framework. He accepts what he finds, though only after examining the multifaceted viewpoints of an argument or of himself. This acceptance already obviates vanity. Montaigne comes to grip with this apparent destroyer of knowledge in the third book in one of the longer essays he wrote, "Of Vanity" (111: 12).

The elliptical allusion to vanity with which the essay starts can be construed as a means to avoid the issue or even dispose of it; the omission of the word at first may indicate a timid stance toward it, but in fact this absence foreshadows its defeat: "There is none aimlessly more obvious than to write of it so vainly. What the divinity has so divinely told us about it ought to be carefully and continually meditated by people of understanding" (p. 721).[4] And of course Montaigne is precisely one of those "people of understanding" who has spent a good part of his life meditating on the question of knowing and writing about it, in spite of divine admonitions. This enterprise of writing explains the predominance of the metaphor of the voyage, the spiritual pilgrimage, in this essay in the face of the metaphoric undercurrent of the physician and sickness and the vanity of household chores, concern with the materialistic life. Then the essay ends with Montaigne's pride in having been made a citizen of Rome, and he cites in full the pagelong Latin proclamation which makes him a citizen of the world; by implication, then, he suggests the universality of his *Essays,* a just but not exactly a humble pretension. The essay dealing squarely with vanity refutes vanity. Montaigne pretends to write vainly in an essay which is not vain. Or is it, as the end implies? The answer Montaigne would like best is yes and no. At any rate, if vanity obfuscates knowledge, it also becomes its source in the limited way that knowing is possible. Every absolute is reduced to a profitable function.

The degree of knowledge is further delimited by fortune. Chance may take on a geographic face, for a notion acceptable in one place may not be so in another, and only the accident of location gives an idea or a belief its validity. Time can play a similar role; an idea accepted during one century can be reversed during the next. This impact of fortune, of the accident of space and time, brings to the fore above all the arbitrariness of this agent that challenges human intelligence. Indeed, the question of fortune preoccupied the humanists because it paralleled inquiry with the very core of man's existence and his relation to his universe. The inexplicable act that often shatters life, is it a manifestation of God's wrath against man's sinful existence? Or is it some supernatural force that strikes blindly at random and which he must endure to the best of his ability and from which he may even gain in stature? Two centuries before Montaigne the two guiding lights of humanism faced this question, one using the metaphor of the plague. Boccaccio reflects on the dilemma in the prologue to his *Decameron,* and Petrarch devotes a whole Latin work to it, *De Remediis Utriusque Fortunae.* To the ancients, of course, fortune appeared often as an implacable and foreordained fate that reduces man to a floundering object. In a Christian light the relationship between free will and predestination deals with an identical problem.

Montaigne does not pretend to offer any solution to this multifaceted question. In fact, he never actually comes to serious grips with it; he ascertains, reflects, accepts it, but does not consider it in a systematic manner or as an integral part of a fundamental philosophical problem. Instead, it appears for the most part in the context of the vagaries of human comprehension, action and creativity:

> Now, I say that not only in medicine but in many more certain arts Fortune has a large part. Poetic sallies, which transport their author and ravish him out of himself, why shall we not attribute them to his good luck? . . . But Fortune shows still more evidently the part she has in all these works by the graces and beauties that are found in them, not only without the workman's intention, but even without his knowledge . . . .
>
> As for military enterprises, everyone sees how large a part Fortune has in them. Even in our counsels and our deliberations there must certainly be some chance and good luck mixed in; for all that our wisdom can do is not much; the sharper and livelier it is, the more weakness it finds in itself and the more it mistrusts itself. I am of Sulla's opinion; when I scrutinize closely the most glorious exploits of war, I see, it seems to me, that those who conduct them make use of deliberation and counsel only for form; they abandon the better part of the enterprise to Fortune, and, in the confidence they have in her help, go beyond the limits of all reason at every turn. (I: 24, 93)

This positive and creative abandonment to fortune holds on to the very last essays (cf. III: 5, 668). Fortune is no longer an exception, but the norm and an integral part of the human experience. A concept of faith and divine providence can replace the more pagan Fortune (cf. the "Apology," II: 12, 375) with the same compliant result and provide a solution to the fortuitous without explaining its cause, however. On the whole, then, because of the arbitrariness and ominous presence of fortune, Montaigne admits to another failure of knowing and its causal role, and advocates therefore an acceptance of the accidents of life, time and space, if not a dependence on them.

III *The Inadequacy of Language*

A major obstacle to knowing is language itself. For the most part, Montaigne contends, a discrepancy exists between what the word says and what it means, between the meaning of the word and the object it designates: "There is the name and the thing. The name is a sound which designates and signifies the thing; the name is not a part of the thing or of the substance, it is an extraneous piece attached to the thing, and outside of it" (II : 16, 468). Language then, in the ordinary form we use, is inadequate to express ourselves; it can only convey a semblance of our thoughts, enfeebled because of the arbitrary significance attributed to a word or because of the various connotations a word may have in other minds.[5] This deficiency of expressive tools would usually call for the forging of a new language, but Montaigne instead will choose to transform the existing one into his own.

The inadequacy of words faces each prose writer or poet, and most bridge the gap between word and meaning by imparting more than one accepted meaning to an identical word; some will invent parts of a totally new language, like Rabelais and Joyce. In Montaigne's case, his skepticism can explain his questioning attitude toward words; after all, a linguistic doubt does cause an ideological one, and he may have found this correlation in Sextus Empiricus, a leading skeptic whom he read and admired. Furthermore, Plato's *Cratylus*, not unknown to Montaigne, posits the same abyss between the word and its designated object. During the Middle Ages, this ongoing linguistic question pits the "realists" against the "nominalists." The realists hold that universal notions really exist, and the words used to express them reflect their meaning; whereas the nominalists claim that these universals are a mere figment of man's imagination, arbitrarily designated by words. And in his own times, Montaignes's linguistic stance continues a quarrel against empty rhetoric begun by Erasmus at the beginning of the century. The author of *In Praise of Folly* strikes out against Ciceronianism as it could manifest itself if labored excessively, that is, a vacuous facade of syntax and words propping up a specious edifice of meaning. Although maintaining an identical position, Montaigne still realizes the strengths and weaknesses of language; after all, language remains the only means to communicate, and the solution lies in harnessing it and transforming it. Silence does not offer the solution to learning to know himself and having others know him.

From the beginning to the end of the *Essays,* Montaigne maintains the emptiness of words that reflects an inherent inevitable failure of knowledge and communication, due to the discrepancy between the noun and the object it designates, and an abusive treatment of words. He pictures, therefore, intellectual pursuits and the

quest for knowledge as a battle of words; man engages in this idle
task because he refuses to face essential matters and prefers to
lose himself in superficialities and games. Of course, Montaigne
is not totally guiltless of these accusations, nor does he attempt
to deny them; though a smile may be present here too: "The world
is nothing but babble, and I never saw a man who did not say
rather more than less than he should. And yet half of our life is
wasted on that . . . . It is more of a job to interpret the interpretations than to interpret the things, and there are more books about
books than about any other subject: we do nothing but write
glosses about each other. The world is swarming with commentaries;
of authors there is a great scarcity" (I: 26, 124; III: 13, 818).

To combat this inflated eloquence, Montaigne proposes a
natural language that would narrow the abyss between word and
meaning. He equates excessive eloquence with flattery and advocates
a demystified and lean language, the kind he claims he himself has:

I have neither the faculty nor the taste for those lengthy offers of affection
and service. I do not really believe all that, and I dislike saying much of
anything beyond what I believe. That is a far cry from the present practice,
for there never was so abject and servile a prostitution of complimentary
addresses: life, soul, devotion, adoration, serf, slave, all these words
have such vulgar currency . . . . I mortally hate to seem a flatterer; and so
I naturally drop into a dry, plain, blunt way of speaking, which, to any
one who does not know me otherwise, verges a little on the disdainful."
(I: 40, 186)

Does Montaigne believe everything he says? Does he always
express himself in a "dry, plain, blunt way"? To what extent can
he be different from other men who are "being accustomed to
speak false words" and who "have no scruples about breaking
their word" (II: 17, 491)? Because breaking one's word and breaking
words are part and parcel of speaking and writing.

A word per se means nothing, and yet on the other hand, it is
everything. Consider the name Montaigne. Although nearly
ubiquitous and despite Montaigne's claim to the contrary, it
overcomes its intrinsic shallowness and meaninglessness and
acquires an identity by becoming applicable to an individual:
"I have no name that is sufficiently my own. Of two that I have,
one is common to my whole race, and indeed to others also. There
is a family in Paris and one in Montpellier named Montaigne,

another in Brittany and in Saintonge called de la Montaigne. The change of a single syllable will tangle our threads so that I will share in their glory, and they, perhaps, in my shame" (II: 16, 475). Somehow the linguistic juggling does not convince. The arbitrariness of an insignificant name loses its vacuous status precisely when word and individual coalesce; even if this fortuitous coupling can change, the argument remains more speculative than effective because Michel de Montaigne persists.

In fact, the word attains a relatively supreme position because man can resort to no other tool to express himself. It suffers some inherent drawback caused as much by human failings to manage it as by intrinsic ambiguity. Hence, in spite of protestations to the contrary, never abandoned because the inquiry must continue, the divinity of the word is proclaimed; in the end then, not the word but its manipulator or exorciser is being tested:

> Since mutual understanding is brought about solely by way of words, he who breaks his word betrays human society. It is the only instrument by means of which our wills and thoughts communicate, it is the interpreter of our soul. If it fails us, we have no more hold on each other, no more knowledge of each other. If it deceives us, it breaks up all our relations and dissolves all the bonds of our society." (II: 18, 505)

The umbilical cord among men, between Montaigne and his *Essays,* must not be broken. In spite of the word's splintering effects, it remains the only possible cohesive factor of communication. The bond/break dichotomy obsesses the Renaissance and reflects its spiritual crisis: the break with the Middle Ages and the bond with antiquity, the relations among men and between man and woman, especially in lyric poetry, and in this labyrinth the word is the fallible medium.

The inherent weakness of the word lies in its lack of precision and in its multiple connotations; at the same time this fluidity also provides the basis for its strength, because a word acquires multidimensional possibilities for the writer to express himself, and he can even shield himself behind this linguistic ambivalence. Even though in the very last essay Montaigne protests the inadequacy of words, he is not so much setting forth a self-apology or a frustration as he is suggesting the potential malleability of words which he himself has masterfully exhibited; and this fluid linguistic condition is inextricably tied with the flaws inherent to satisfactory knowledge:

Our disputes are purely verbal. I ask what is "nature," "pleasure," "circle," "substitution." The question is one of words, and is answered in the same way. "A stone is a body." But if you pressed on: "And what is a body?"— "Substance."—"And what is substance?" and so on, you would finally drive the respondent to the end of the lexicon. We exchange one word for another word, often more unknown. I know better what is man than I know what is animal, or mortal, or rational. To satisfy one doubt, they give me three; it is the Hydra's head.

Socrates asked Meno what virtue was. "There is," said Meno, "the virtue of a man and a woman, of a magistrate and of a private individual, of a child and of an old man." "That's fine," exclaimed Socrates; "we were in search of one virtue, and here is a whole swarm of them." (III: 13, 818–19)

The word encompasses the metamorphoses of intellectual life; it lays bare discriminating layers of knowledge according to interpretations of its various meaning. Indeed, a further debilitation or, on the other hand, revitalization of the word occurs when it leaves the one who has spoken or written it and reaches the other party. At this point it acquires a status that is independent of its creator and at the mercy of the receptor.

Although spoken or imprinted language has a crystallized, stable, and fixed quality, it still reflects the movements and shapes of the human mind and its experiences and remains subject to a quartering by those from whom it emanates and by those on the receiving end: "Speech belongs half to the speaker, half to the listener. The latter must prepare to receive it according to the motion it takes. As among tennis players, the receiver moves and makes ready according to the motion of the striker and the nature of the stroke" (III: 13, 834). Aware of this duality, Montaigne adapts to it, exploits it, and even makes it a basic tenet of his *Essays;* the creation of a metaphoric language imitating the daily common language and fragmenting words through their multiple connotations blends with and reinforces an incessant inquiry and an unsettled thinking, thus achieving a fusion of form and content.

Irrespective of their failings, a writer must master words. He does so by having them become a part of him. In the process they ought to lose some of their fluidity and autonomous identity. Montaigne then succeeds in amalgamating words to his thought by imparting to them a specific metaphoric dimension; at the same time, however, he loses control over them as soon as they leave him and begin working on the reader's imagination. The ultimate life of the word therefore lies between the writer's incorporating it, attempting to fix it, and the reader's imagination that fragments and dissolves it:

There are some men so stupid that they go a mile out of their way to chase after a fine word, *or who do not fit words to things, but seek irrelevant things which their words may fit* [Quintilian]. And as another says, *There are some who are led by the charm of some attractive word to write something they had not intended.* [Seneca]. I much more readily twist a good saying to sew it on me than I twist the thread of my thought to go fetch it. On the contrary, it is for words to serve and follow; and let Gascon get there if French cannot. I want the substance to stand out, and so to fill the imagination of the listener that he will have no memory of the words. (I: 26, 127)

Montaigne aims at the creation of a metaphoric language that will diminish the distance between word and object by focusing on "substance," meaning, and concept. But can he succeed if the distance between the reader and the word remains? All he can do is to formulate a language that comes from within him, that has been "sewn" on to him; meanwhile the vacuum, or the plenitude of words, will fill pages. In just this way Mallarmé was aware of and tortured by a creative sterility but kept on composing poems on this subject, because creative limitations, linguistic and imaginative, provide the very impulse to creation, the attempt to resolution.

IV   *Sincerity, Playfulness and Irony*

The question of Montaigne's sincerity further embarrasses a concept of assured knowledge which the *Essays* for the most part rejects, although there is more chance of succeeding in knowing the self than in understanding the outside world. When is Montaigne smiling and when does he mean what he says? He certainly entices the reader and enjoys leading him astray. He indulges in frequent deprecation of himself and his writings, but to what extent does he mean it? Montaigne could also be accused of dilettantism. Like a gadfly he picks and chooses what suits him without a prolonged involvement in any one path; yet it is this very process that forms him, that makes him what he is, and produces his self-awareness and self-knowledge. A refusal to wear only one mask allows freedom of action and change and leaves all options open, for ultimately Montaigne advocates the availability of the self to any natural desire. What can be construed as dilettantism, then, is not mere dabbling, but becomes an integral part of the substance of the *Essays* and its purpose. The apparently playful dilettantism has all the trappings and functions of the paradox, a curiosity and diversion of the mind. Or is it a deceptive game to snare and confuse the reader? A case could be made for both view-points, and a smiling Montaigne stands above it all.

A sense of play does exist in the *Essays,* and it effects more the relationship between it and the reader than between Montaigne and his work. It reflects a contrivance and manipulation of ideas that bring about the very opposite of what was being purported, or it challenges credibility beyond a reasonable point. In the "Apology of Raymond Sebond," for example, Montaigne sets out to show the equality of animals with men, or even their superiority, but the argument takes on such enormous proportions, as the cases are enumerated page after page, that the overabundant rhetoric puts the conviction in jeopardy. Animals may behave very much like men and even exhibit as much reason and intellect, but the avalanche of examples and their often exceptional quality erase both their credibility and their impact on the argument.

The resulting empty rhetoric further downgrades human reason, one of the principal aims of the essay. Montaigne acknowledges that he has gone astray by this huge accumulation of examples, and feigns to return to the main thrust of his case, the weakness of man; in an overt show of irony, he proceeds to suggest that man may still be superior to animals because of a certain category of traits that distinguish them: "But to return to my subject, we have as our share inconstance, irresolution, uncertainty, grief, super-stition, worry over things to come even after our life, ambition, avarice, jealousy, envy, unruly, frantic, and untamable appetites, war, falsehood, disloyalty, detraction, and curiosity" (p. 358). This list aims at disparaging man and his passions, for the traits in reality continue to make him inferior to animals while seeming to give him a superiority. Yet some of these human characteristics are at the very core of human consciousness, which gives a meaning to life and indeed to man a tragic superiority over animal: in-constance, irresolution, uncertainty, grief, afterlife, and above all, curiosity, that humanistic deity.

At what point does one pin Montaigne down? One senses a trace of playfulness in his quest for knowledge. Are we really sure, though? Because too often he slithers away and leaves the reader holding the bag. He could answer, however, that those who play are the ones who pretend to solve insoluble philosophical questions. He himself likes to undermine his own position and the supposed purpose of an essay. The "Apology for Raymond Sebond" (II: 12) aims at exposing the fallibility of reason; yet Montaigne uses reason as the bludgeoning weapon. Many an essay cancels itself out. "Of Liars" (I: 9) purports to take a position against lying, but truth has no fewer faces than lying and vice versa. "Of Vain Subtleties" (I: 54) can be construed as the very essence of the *Essays* that attempts to dissect an argument into its fine points and not necessarily as a procedural drawback. "Of Moderation" (I: 30) makes a strong case for the opposite. An essay starts out in one direction but ends up in another, or at least has deviated from its initial aim. Does Montaigne create obstacles to show us and himself that he can overcome them? A case can be made for the player in search of intellectual games. In this vein, one critic points out the game Montaigne plays with pronouns. In the same paragraph he will switch from *I* to *we,* on the one hand, and then from *one* to *they* on the other hand, in the midst of a discussion. The *we* and *they* reflect customary opinions pitted against the *I,* and its possible errors or illusions, but the *we* also includes the *I* and clouds, therefore, any objective separation, as the *I* slips into the *we* against the *they.*[6] The observed and the observer become fused with the opinions of others and the self, in an inextricable fashion that defies certitude.

The question of Montaigne's sincerity remains problematic. Of course, both possible opinions exist. Some hold that he truly attempts to depict himself as he sees himself—complex and often contradictory, and therefore a reflection or embodiment of a similar outside world of things and knowledge.[7] Others declare that Montaigne should not be taken seriously at any time, for a smile always lurks in the background.[8] Perhaps Montaigne himself, if he were asked, would answer that a self-portrait cannot be entirely objective; furthermore, others do not see him as he saw himself, or thought he saw himself. In his effort to present a universalized self-portrait, does he not draw a somewhat idealized picture of himself that does not hide minor vices but does not reveal major ones either? In face the *Essays* is not a diary nor a genuine confession, but rather a reflection on the self and the universe in which it had to live. Hence, how can we know that Montaigne was really such as he describes himself?

An evergrowing critical consensus sees an ironic strain in the *Essays*. Although this view derives from an interpretation of the essays, it is also in accord with the prevalent literary technique of the Renaissance.[9] The reason irony appealed so much to the Renaissance mind is that, in the Socratic sense of the word, it was simulation of ignorance. Saying something and meaning or insinuating something else compel the reader to wonder and to question. When Montaigne with a smiling exaggeration simulates incompetence in everyday matters—in handling money, in household affairs, in agriculture—or when he depreciates his role as mayor, the reader has to rectify and reconcile in his mind good faith and feint. This kind of irony allows for a certain flexibility of thought on Montaigne's part and indicates an incertitude. Or is it a form of vanity? If one accepts a smile by Montaigne, does it mean that he refuses to take the world seriously or that he resigns himself to it without much hope? Or is he a mere observer who amuses himself with the contradictory facets of life, thus communicating both his skepticism and an enjoyment of living?[10] Yet Montaigne does wipe away his smile before he dogmatizes, and he is as ready to show himself dogmatic against dogmatisms as to use irony to undermine a secure position: "It may be said with some plausibility that there is an abecedarian ignorance that comes before knowledge, and another, doctoral ignorance that comes after knowledge: an ignorance that knowledge creates and engenders, just as it undoes and destroys the first" (I: 54, 227).

V *Self-Depreciation and Nonchalance*

One of Montaigne's favorite games is self-depreciation.[11] He disparages both himself and his essays. However, when he downgrades himself, he directs his jabs more at self-portrayal than at self-study. At the beginning, this self-depreciation may indeed indicate a lack of self-assurance in face of the task he has undertaken, and an uncertainty concerning the reception of his labors; at this stage a measure of sincerity could very well punctuate this kind of remark:

> This also happens to me: that I do not find myself in the place where I look; and I find myself more by chance encounter than by searching my judgment. I will have tossed off some subtle remark as I write. (I mean, of course, dull for anyone else, sharp for me. But let's leave aside all these amenities. Each man states this kind of thing according to his powers). Later I have lost the point so thoroughly that I do not know what I meant; and sometimes a stranger has discovered it before I do. If I erased every passage where this happens to me, there would be nothing left to myself. (I: 11, 26–27)

But as this self-depreciation occurs with increasing frequency, especially in the third book, and also exhibits a disparaging vocabulary, the irony emerges even though an interplay between sincerity and irony lingers on. When Montaigne refers to his essays as "some excrements of an aged mind, now hard, now loose, and always undigested" (III: 9, 721), or "This fricassee that I am scribbling here" (III, 13, 826), he both scorns and praises his task. He smiles at himself and sets a trap for the reader who will take him literally; yet the *Essays,* on the surface, does fit the description he gives of it. Any trace of modesty present at the beginning disappears under the weight of a later false modesty. He lowers himself to rise better above the others, to stress his uniqueness in spite of his success at universality.

Montaigne is aware of the difficulties of knowing, but has no doubt about the inroads he has made. Of course, he has no illusion of total success, and the self-depreciation expresses his limitations within an absolute, but not the validity of his aim. If he becomes more derogatory of himself in his later years, it is actually to veil at times any accomplishment he has attained: "But whatever I make myself known to be, provided I make myself known such as I am, I am carrying out my plan. And so I make no excuse for daring to put into writing such mean and trivial remarks as these. The meanness of my subject forces me to do so. Blame my project if you will, but not my procedure" (II: 17, 495). The last sentence is a post-1588 addition and attests to Montaigne's strong convictions about his enterprise; in fact, the English "procedure" is *progrez* in French. However, the path is a tortuous one.

Self-depreciation indicates also self-criticism. Montaigne himself is his own foremost intransigent reader, and because he explores and discovers more than the reader would, he protects himself through a game of acting foolish. Furthermore, he pretends not to

believe in what he deals with in order to look at it more objectively
and to renew this subject matter of knowing; the process of down-
grading it gives an opportunity to revive it, often in a different
light.

Self-depreciation is transformed into an aesthetics of negligence.[12] In this vein, Montaigne wants to appear to convey a
a sense of nonchalance by casting off carelessly, on the surface,
contradictory notions, by giving the impression of structuring an
essay aimlessly, on the surface again, by ending many an essay in
a whimsical or unexpected way. The purpose of this pseudonegli-
gence is to create a climate of open-endedness which in turn reflects
a world in constant flux and Montaigne's absolute subjectivity,
prone to incessant change. The most significant manifestation
of this aesthetics of negligence is the apparent offhandness with
which the author handles an essay, so that he can no longer be
held entirely responsible for the meanings it assumes for the reader,
irrespective of what Montaigne intended. This position serves
as an escape hatch in the case of controversial passages, but above
all it suggests potential multiple meanings and advances a challenge—and a trap—for the reader: "Those actions have much
more grace which escape from the hand of the workman nonchalantly and noiselessly, and which some worthy man later
picks out and lifts back out of obscurity to push them into the
light for their own sake" (III: 10, 783). This cultivated negligence
belongs to the Renaissance; Petrarch, Castiglione, Tasso, Rabelais
strongly favor it.[13] Montaigne finds it invaluable because it fits
in with a primordial concept of the *Essays* as a composite, sometimes
ineffable, unity that is all-embracing. With a wink, he nudges the
reader out of a chaotic state into a state of limited knowledge:
"This stuffing is a little out of my subject. I go out of my way, but
rather by license than carelessness. My ideas follow one another,
but sometimes it is from a distance, and look at each other, but
with a sidelong glance" (III: 9, 761).

VI   *Whither Memory?*

Nonchalance, an aesthetics of negligence, or a further clear
attempt at mystification, takes on a semblance of a lack of memory.
Montaigne claims forgetfulness in order to play the game of ignorance, to distinguish himself from others (pedants), and to rein-

force self-depreciation. Significantly enough, the first mention of this lack of memory occurs in a very early essay, "Of Liars" (I : 9), in the context of telling the truth—hence, knowing. Although Montaigne deplores his shortcoming, he still views it as a distinction "worthy of gaining a name and reputation" (p. 21). What concerns him in retrospect is that his unique fault has not been taken at its face value and that he has been accused of parading it to placate his lack of judgment and decision:

> But they do me wrong. For rather the opposite is seen by experience: that excellent memories are prone to be joined to feeble judgment. They do me wrong also in this, I who know how to do nothing so well as be a friend: that by the very words they use to denounce my malady they also make me look ungrateful. They blame my feelings for my want of memory, and of a natural lack they make a lack of conscience . . . . Certainly I may easily forget, but careless about the charge with which my friend has entrusted me, that I am not. Let them be content with my infirmity, without making it into a sort of malice, and a malice so alien to my nature. (I : 9, 22)

The claim to the supposed lack of memory makes the writing down of his thought, of the *Essays,* all the more necessary; therein lies the ploy and the game of this kind of protestation. Montaigne complains that he cannot memorize even three verses, but he has no difficulty acting in plays. The essays then become a substitute for avoiding forgetfulness, or the very positive substance resulting from this so-called natural vice, yet a distinctive uniqueness; and if remembering can inadvertently lead to lying, then forgetting may produce a kind of truth. Eventually the question assumes an aesthetic and epistemological dimension; a natural flaw is replaced by an artificial quality and artful endeavor. If to know is hindered through natural means, then an attempt will be made through an artificial memory: "For lack of a natural memory I make one of paper" (III : 13, 837).

Because memory is "so feeble an instrument" (III : 9, 735), Montaigne must not fall prey to pedantry, namely, an excessive dependence on others that obfuscates the core of argument. He will use his lack of memory judiciously. He does not deny this dependence on others forced on him by his forgetfulness, but at the same time he draws away from them and asserts that knowing retains its validity only in relation to the present and not the past: "I go about cadging from books here and there the sayings that please me, not to keep them, for I have no storehouses, but to transport them into this one, in which, to tell the truth, they are no more mine than in their original place. We are, I believe, learned only with present knowledge, not with past, any more than with future" (I: 25, 100). Again Montaigne wishes to stress the different quality of his work; his *Essays* is not a mere pedantic compilation of examples and sentences occasioned by lack of memory, since these sources are transformed into a new and personalized form of knowledge. And besides, since forgetfulness can lead to contradictions, a dependence on one's own judgment is a much safer crutch to lean on (I: 9; II: 17). This last finding allows for a trace of a smile, just as when later in life Montaigne complains that his growing lack of memory causes repetitions in his essays (III: 9, 734-35); of course, he never repeats himself, but following his peripatetic stylistic course, he simply views the same object or argument from a different vantage point in time and space.

No matter how much Montaigne complains of his supposed lack of memory, in fact he neither needs it nor wants it in order to retain a variety of options of action and thought. For this reason he pretends to remain independent of it in the guise of a lack of it, or rather, he makes a controlled use of it in the guise of a nonchalant relationship with it: "Now, the more I distrust my memory, the more confused it becomes. It serves me better by chance encounter; I have to solicit it nonchalantly. For if I press it, it is stunned; and once it has begun to totter, the more I probe it, the more it gets mixed up and embarrassed. It serves me at its own time, not at mine" (II: 17, 493). If he claimed to adhere strictly to a rigid memory, the whole ambivalent edifice of self-depreciation would come tumbling down and with it his hard-core conviction of the difficulty of attaining knowledge. This specific form of a sometimes playful self-denigration provides him with another dimension of mobility which he must have. He complains of a lack of memory from which he does not suffer in order to explain and implicitly praise a meandering thought and style that depends on a process of recall, artificial though it may be at times.

Lest the reader delude himself, the *Essays* could not exist without memory. The instrument to seize time, things, being, knowledge, in any possible measure, is memory by means of natural recall or by association in order to shape a permanent paper memory. Montaigne's natural memory is what Proust calls his conscious memory, and the associative memory is the equivalent of Proust's unconscious memory. The two processes of recall lead to an identical result: the artificial paper memory that substantiates the *Essays* and the deification of Art that constitutes one of the rationales for *In Remembrance of Things Past*. This artificial memory gains ascendency because collective memory, like individual memory, fails, and then it is the responsibility of a self-appointed leader to become the custodian of time, to keep a register of events, to bring to light from the morass of time works and deeds of men that will serve as models to emulate. To seize the past means to conquer the future, to realize the position and the privilege of a leader through a memory of paper:

> Of so many myriads of valiant men who have died sword in hand in the last fifteen hundred years in France, there are not a hundred who have come to our knowledge. The memory not only of the leaders, but of the battles and victories, is buried.
> The fortunes of more than half the world, for lack of a record, do not stir from their place, and vanish without duration. If I had in my possession all the unknown events, I should think I could very easily supplant those that are known, in every kind of examples . . . . It will be a lot if a hundred years from now people remember in a general way that in our time there were civil wars in France . . . . We have not the thousandth part of the writings of the ancients: it is Fortune that gives them life, longer or shorter according to her favor; and it is permissible to wonder whether what we have is not the worst, since we have not seen the rest. People do not write histories about such petty things. A man must have been the leader in conquering an empire or a kingdom; he must have won fifty-two pitched battles, always with weaker numbers, like Caesar. (II: 16, 475–76)

Even the more durable paper memory has its limitations; it captures only fragments and attempts to transmute them into a new whole. Under the circumstances, it is the best possible method, since imperfection is inherent to knowledge. Indeed, memory operates in the context of the uncertainty of knowledge. On the one hand, the lack of memory is ignorance; on the other hand, the power to recall, in spite of its shortcomings, is the act through which the mind asserts itself and battles the "weaker numbers." Montaigne claims the former, but adheres to the latter, in order to become a Caesar, a powerful station in life dependent on the weakness of others.[14]

VII   *The Conquest of Time*

"There is no desire more natural than the desire for knowledge"
(III: 13, 815), but time hinders this pursuit because it undermines
stability and certainty. There are two notions of time, an exterior
one that reflects the world about us and its changing and flighty
nature, and an inner one that results from a concept of duration
and leads to psychological time and continuity. The succession of
events or cumulative knowledge on a temporal plan, then, makes
credible the validity of duration or continuity; only a concept of
continuity can redeem the instability and flight of time and master
this evasiveness. Because of its mobility, exterior time invalidates
the past, the future, and even the present:

> For time is a mobile thing, which appears as in a shadow, together with
> matter, which is ever running and flowing, without ever remaining stable
> or permanent. To which belong the words *before* and *after*, and *has been*
> and *will be*, which at the very first sight show very evidently that time is
> not a thing that is; for it would be a great stupidity and a perfectly apparent
> falsehood to say that that is which is not yet in being; or which already has
> ceased to be. And for these words, *present, immediate, now*, on which it
> seems that we chiefly found and support our understanding of time, reason
> discovering this immediately destroys it; for she at once splits and divides
> it into the future and past, as though wanting to see it necessarily divided
> in two. (II: 12, 456)

Time about us follows an inexorable pattern, and man can do
nothing to alter its course. Any attempt to harness this time and
make it fit human activity remains futile and artificial; on the
contrary, man must realize a consonance with the mutability of
time: "It is two or three years since they shortened the year by ten
days in France. How many changes were supposed to follow this
reform! It was literally moving heaven and earth at the same time.
Nevertheless there is nothing budging from its place . . . . Neither
was the error felt in our habits, nor is the improvement. So much
uncertainty there is in all things; so gross, obscure, and obtuse
is our perception!" (III: 11, 784). In spite of its cyclical nature,
time remains impervious to man; he must simply submit to it, to
its appearances at least. Yet to assert himself and feign a measure
of knowledge, he must conquer it. This task may be impossible
if limited to the outer mobility of time, but not so if concentrated
on its inner essence that man can assimilate, the instant.

Seen in the light of time, the *Essays* attempts to reconcile the concept of duration, inherent to it, with the instant in order to overcome temporal mobility. Duration means an awareness of the succession of events and experiences, hence the changing nature of time; or rather time becomes the agent of change. This consciousness produces an experiential and historical continuity, pointing to mutability and diversity, that not only links the past to the present, but hearkens to the past, while the future receives less attention. Continuity does not necessarily imply a progressive and systematic continuum; on the contrary, it reveals often an accumulation of disparate moments, on the surface at least. Duration, then, becomes the source of a constant creative renewal that redeems temporal mutability and gives primacy to the moment, since one can seize satisfactorily only the instant and not an aggregate of instants. Thus Montaigne does not intend to capture duration, but to create and observe it in its development.

The consciousness of time does not exist for its own sake, but in function of knowledge: self-awareness and the epistemological quest. The ultimate manifestation of time is life in its present state, not as an abstraction but as a substance: how one uses and spends time. Of course, the layers of the past will have an impress on the present; however, only the latter is judged: "The advantage of living is not measured by length, but by use; some men have lived long, and lived little; attend to it while you are in it" (I: 20, 67). The manner of spending time is directly related to the degree of being, self-awareness, and well-being one enjoys:

I have a vocabulary all my own. I "pass the time," when it is raining and disagreeable; when it is good, I do not want to pass it; I savor it, I cling to it. We must run through the bad and settle on the good. This ordinary expression "pastime" or "pass the time" represents the habit of those wise folk who think they can make no better use of their life than to let it slip by and escape it, pass it by, sidestep it, and, as far as in them lies, ignore it and run away from it, as something irksome and contemptible. But I know it to be otherwise and find it both agreeable and worth prizing, even in its last decline, in which I now possess it . . . . However, I am reconciling myself to the thought of losing it, without regret, but as something that by its nature must be lost . . . (III: 13, 853)

Time has become the essence of life; it could reach this existential level only after passing through an experiential stage premised on a belief in continuity and a commitment to the past.

Montaigne' does not intend to provide a systematic explanation of time, nor does he wish to propound a theory of time; he does not aim at understanding it, but at adapting himself to it. Since time means change or is the agent for change, whether considered in the perspective of the past or in the context of the present, Montaigne opts for the immutable instant which alone can be seized, controlled, and understood as much as possible; he reduces therefore temporality to a concentrated essence which focuses on living life on a daily basis and fuses time with the body and the intellect: "Let us manage our time; we shall still have a lot left idle and ill spent. Our mind likes to think it has not enough leisure hours to do its own business unless it dissociates itself from the body for the little time that the body really needs it" (III: 13, 856). Time, then, is considered in the light of pleasure and desires and of the mastery that has to be exercised over them, not just in the last book of the *Essays* but in all three. With time focused on the present, one can give in to a plenitude of life, sustain its continuity, while limiting and controlling desires whenever deemed necessary by reason or by age. Only the present allows for a true consciousness of the self, for being and the possession and limited knowledge of the self. However, the success attained on the ontological and epicurean levels in the present does not occur on the epistemological level; here, between the motion of things and the motion of thought, a temporal hiatus is formed that denies continuity. Time, therefore, permits an interior knowledge but not an exterior one.

On a temporal level it could be argued that the *Essays* moves from the past to the present, from a dependence on history to an emphasis on personal experience that culminates with the last essay bearing this title. Again this shift is a matter of stress and does not imply the appearance of one and the disappearance of another. History means the past, but it also evidences a cumulative process of events, a duration that never ends its onward movement, and upon which the present is built. For Montaigne, this temporal curve does not reflect a systematic or scientific process, but a succession of events often distorted by other men, because he realizes the near impossibility of objectivity in historians. And when in "Of Cannibals" he claims to have found such a dispassionate source, there may very well be a twinkle in his eye:

... for clever people observe more things and more curiously, but they interpret them; and to lend weight and conviction to their interpretation, they cannot help altering history a little. They never show you things as they are, but bend and disguise them according to the way they have seen them; and to give credence to their judgment and attract you to it, they are prone to add something to their matter, to stretch it out and amplify it. We need a man either very honest, or so simple that he has not the stuff to build up false inventions and give them plausibility; and wedded to no theory. Such was my man . . . " (I: 31, 152)

Since history cannot be considered in a static temporal context, and since as a science, an absolute source of knowledge, it contains intrinsic organic drawbacks, Montaigne will use it for its moral didactic purposes. He will study not the events, the actions in time, but the human character and impulse behind the deeds that shape the temporal accident. History then becomes a pool of experiences from which Montaigne chooses according to his needs and even his whim, and the juxtaposition and accumulation of these experiences produce a highly personalized notion of duration, of time. Montaigne, therefore, creates his own arbitrary experiential brand of time that supersedes a falsely objective concept of time.

The citations and the additions to the *Essays* illustrate this individualized notion of time as they reveal either a sharpened distance or a telescoped immediacy with the past. Since a citation or an addition either substantiates or adds another dimension to an argument, presently developed or previously stated, the first function is set against a present and the second one against a relatively immediate past. Each represents an experience and a moral judgment set at a point in time, but their presence and frequence throughout the *Essays,* arranged on an arbitrary basis from a temporal viewpoint, attest to an atemporality which is consciously calculated to conquer the ordinary concept of chronological time. Montaigne does not wish to destroy the past, but to reevaluate it; he offers a critique of time. The successive additions to the essays break down the past somewhat, but do not disintegrate it; Montaigne gives new dimensions to what he has stated previously, without denying anything he has said previously. The use of citations and anecdotes allows Montaigne to manipulate and submit time to his will; he mixes a distant with a more recent past and often lets one contradict another and not necessarily at the expense of the present. There results a dialectic between time and knowledge; on the one hand time produces an uncertainty surrounding knowledge, and on the other it offers the only foundations for any possibility of knowing, because the past, no matter how distant or proximate, to have any validity exists in function of the present. Simultaneously, however, Montaigne creates an atemporality to which he gives precedence by superposing various levels of time into a prismatic narrative that defies time, as we usually conceive it.[15]

VIII   *Consubstantiality*

The uncertainty surrounding knowledge, which time further undermines, apparently disappears in the face of a certainty, that is, the consubstantiality of the *Essays* and its author. The essays form Montaigne, make him what he is, just as Montaigne forms the essays, creates them in his image, so that creator and creation constitute an inseparable and interdependent whole:

Painting myself for others, I have painted my inward self with colors clearer than my original ones. I have no more made my book than my book has made me—a book consubstantial with its author, concerned with my own self, an integral part of my life; not concerned with some third-hand, extraneous purpose, like all other books. Have I wasted my time by taking stock of myself so continually, so carefully? For those who go over themselves only in their minds and occasionally in speech do not penetrate to essentials in their examination as does a man who makes that his study, his work, and his trade, who binds himself to keep an enduring account, with all his faith, with all his strength. (II: 18, 504)

This consubstantiality reveals a certitude about the worthiness of his interprise, irrespective of claims to the contrary that pepper the *Essays;* but, above all, it implies that ultimately everything written down relates to Montaigne, to his thought, his self-portrait, how and why he composes the *Essays.* And he leaves no doubt in "Of the Resemblance of Children to Fathers" (II: 37) that his spiritual and concrete heir is the *Essays,* and he even gives it precedence over any physiological progeny.

An analysis of an early short essay, of slightly more than two pages, "A Trait of Certain Ambassadors" (I: 17), will illustrate how a seemingly tangential topic reflects on Montaigne through a refracting process. To a great extent the essay deals with the use of sources, and he begins by stating that what he extracts from others is what they have an expertise in: "In order always to be learning something by communication with others (which is one of the finest schools there can be), I observe in my travels [writing the *Essays*] this practive: I always steer those I talk with back to the subjects they know best" (p. 49). Of course, he continues, many claim an expertise in matters with which they are usually not associated; for example, Caesar, considered an excellent soldier, also wishes to be remembered as a fine architect, which he was (p. 50). Here Montaigne says others think of him as a magistrate, but he wanted to be known as a fine essayist, like Caesar who "wants to make himself known as an excellent engineer" (p. 50). And although he concludes this argument by advocating that one should exercise his competency within his professional limits and not stray outside of them, because "On that track you never do anything worthwhile" (p. 50), he will still continue as an essayist, since throughout the essays Montaigne pictures himself both in a universal and in a singular and detached light.

To reconcile the two phases of his professional life, the magistrate and the writer, Montaigne chooses for himself a vocation that has an almost universal applicability, and he does so in a somewhat abrupt transition from the question of identity to the apparent subject of the essay; this abruptness gives further evidence of a twinkle in his eye: "Thus we must always throw the architect, the painter, the shoemaker, and the rest each back to his quarry. And apropos of this, in the reading of history, which is everybody's business, I make it a habit to consider who are the authors" (p. 50). He thus lays claim to being a historian of sorts, but a critical one; he views histories from their authors' vantage point and attaches importance only to "what belongs to their business" (p. 50). And so if the author is an ambassador, Montaigne derives from this work the art of "negotiations, understandings, and diplomatic practices, and the way to conduct them" (p. 50). On the surface the transition appears rather rough from the stated purpose of wanting to communicate what one knows best to parading as something which one is not, but which turns out to be more meaningful than what one is supposed to be. Montaigne, then, here takes on the guise of "certain ambassadors," with whom he will associate himself. In other words, he lays claim not to what reflects his expertise, but to what he can relate to himself. Hence no contradiction, really, as long as either vocation aims toward better communication.

Montaigne identifies himself with certain ambassadors because he imparts to them professional traits that he faces in writing essays. When under specific directives, ambassadors ought not to distort the truth in reporting to their chief, as they often do, for they owe obedience to the head of state and any deviation may have counterproductive results, though "We are so eager to get out from under command, under some pretext, and to usurp mastery; each man aspires so naturally to liberty and authority, that to a superior no useful quality in those who serve him should be so dear as their natural and simple obedience" (p. 51). Yet ambassadors ought to have a free hand and use their own judgment as the circumstances dictate; this is the last point Montaigne makes in the essay. In the final analysis, ambassadors remain to a great extent their own masters and much depends on their judgment and their interpretation of events and of what is in the best interest of those they serve: "Ambassadors have a freer commission, which in many areas depends in the last resort on their judgment; they do not simply carry out, but also by their counsel form and direct their master's will" (p. 51). The dilemmas facing the ambassadors are the same as those confronting the writer of the essays as he grapples with the question of how to handle his sources at this point, his readings, the anecdotes and quotations which he uses much more than actual experiences.

Just as the ambassador stands between his master and the event or decision, so Montaigne finds himself between his sources and his prospective reader. Montaigne attempts to decide how faithful he ought to be to his sources. Must he adhere to what they state literally or in context? Or can he interpret them in a manner to fit his argument or the context of the essay? The ambassadors also become the essays themselves in relation to their author and to their meaning. Should they be seen only in a narrow light, or should they be able to move within a flexible spectrum of meaning? The answer is soon quite clear: "Men of understanding still condemn the practice of the kings of Persia, who gave such minutely detailed instructions to their agents and lieutenants that in the slightest matters they had to have recourse to these instructions; so that the resulting delay, in so vast an area of dominion, often did notable harm to their affairs" (p. 51). It becomes apparent, therefore, that in "A Trait [obedience or flexibility] of Certain Ambassadors" Montaigne deals with a moral question, a crisis in professional identity, as he gropes metaphorically with the craft of fiction, with the dilemmas that confront a new writer in search of his métier. This consubstantiality of the questioning writer and his craft, of commitment and alienation, of wrong and and right, good and evil, body and spirit pervades the whole of the *Essays*. If these apparent contradictions are indivisible, so are an evanescent Montaigne and the essays that reflect him; they constitute a whole, one substance; they are consubstantial.

IX   *What Self?*

Consubstantiality, then, is the fusion of what Montaigne is and what he says or writes down. But who is Montaigne? Is the Montaigne that emerges from the *Essays* an exact replica of the Montaigne that actually existed? The safest answer is: not exactly. Montaigne depicts himself much more as he sees himself than as others see him; therefore his self-portrait is bound to lack some objectivity, although this subjectivism does not reduce the validity of the portrait as a created self. Many significant details delineate this portrait, especially toward the end of the *Essays;* yet the composite picture remains impressionistic, difficult to grasp. Even if one accepts this self for what it is, as one should—namely, a valid poetic projection—there still arise a number of antinomies within it. To begin with the authenticity of the portrait, a moot question remains: "Now, I am constantly adorning myself, for I am constantly describing myself" (II: 16, 273). Montaigne seeks to possess an evanescent self. Although the *Essays* is a written confession to a large extent, how much remains unsaid that would alter the writtten portrait? Montaigne claims universality for himself, yet he endeavors repeatedly to rise above the herd, to maintain and cultivate an individuality; humility does not exclude vanity, but to what extent he is suffused with either defies solution: "I consider myself one of the common sort, except in that I consider myself so; guilty of the commoner and humbler faults, but not of faults disavowed or excused; and I value myself for knowing my value. If there is vainglory in me, it is infused in me superficially by the treachery of my nature, and has no body of its own to appear before my judgment. I am sprinkled with it, but not dyed" (II: 17, 481).

To a large extent, the *Essays* is the manifestation of an attempt to possess the self and an apology for that self, often with ironic overtones. Possession of the self means attempts at knowledge.

Yet even the descent into oneself presents difficulties and incertitude, and a degree of anguish at the beginning of the *Essays:* "I have little control over myself and my moods. Chance has more power here than I. The occasion, the company, the very sound of my voice, draw more from my mind than I find in it when I sound it and use it by myself. Thus its speech is better than its writings, if there can be choice where there is no value" (I: 10, 26). The study of the self results from an awareness of the difficulty of attaining knowledge, and the self therefore becomes the conscience that judges and attempts to decipher an interior chaos. Because of a pervasive flux, the possession of the self remains ephemeral, so that the quest for knowledge alternates endlessly between a momentary revelation and an incessant pursuit.

The challenges and contradictions that the self offered at the beginning persist to the very end, but by then Montaigne has become reconciled to them through the evaluation and observation of the cumulative process that has taken place. The real self that has emerged is the one created in the *Essays,* and whether it duplicates faithfully or fully the Montaigne that lived remains questionable, if not irrelevant; it is much more self-observation than self-depiction. Still, to the last, Montaigne never takes the easy road; the self may form an organic unity, but it always leaves room for further search in spite of outer serenity. In fact, the study of the self is the generative and creative force within Montaigne that defies his inevitable submission to the universe.

To abandon the body is not to abandon the mind, which continues to delve within itself; the self has now realized its potential and its limits as it looks back upon the layers it has constructed of itself. In spite of its disparateness, the self has integrated with its surroundings through awareness of its uniqueness and its universality and by accepting the impossibility of knowing:

In this universe of things I ignorantly and negligently let myself by guided by the general law of the world. I shall know it well enough when I feel it. My knowledge could not make it change its path; it will not modify itself for me. It is folly to hope it, and greater the folly to be troubled about it, since it is necessarily uniform, public, and common . . . . I would rather be an authority on myself than on Cicero. In the experience I have of myself I find enough to make me wise, if I were a good scholar . . . . Let us only listen: we tell ourselves all we most need. (III: 13, 821)

One purpose of studying the self is to arrive at a spiritual lucidity, a consciousness of being, a realization that knowing the self, hence in a way any measure also of epistemology, is a most feasible endeavor and yet not totally fulfilled. From this partial failure issues a 'quest for authenticity accompanied by a parallel mask which is just as valid as another self because the search for the self produces many selves. Yet this particular exploration should not be construed as mere introspection during which Montaigne loses himself, but more as a controlled multifaceted exposition that blurs the line of demarcation between true and false. This detached observation leads to an urge for further composition, writing, to a fragmentation of the self that is thereby neutralized within its diversified components; similarly, the resulting knowledge of the self backs away from any polarity. Because in the final analysis whatever applies to the knowledge of the self, to ontology,' applies equally to epistemology, the knowledge of the exterior world; in the *Essays,* the study of the self is the metaphor for the quest for knowledge, and the praise of individuality contains not only an encomium of universality, but the portrait of both a participant and a spectator, Montaigne.

X   *Glory and Posterity*

If knowledge remains problematic within the context of the self and of the outside world, there must be some additional rationale behind the writing of the *Essays.* Could it be that Montaigne wants to leave a trace of himself, a record of his thought processes, a monument that would attest to a hope for explicit or implicit glory? Some readers of the *Essays* may feel that Montaigne had no such intent, for he does condemn displays of vanity and the need for glory as empty bags of wind, but he takes care to differentiate between one type of glory and another, between an empty one and a meaningful one. The humanist of the Renaissance—and this category encompasses all men of letters—carried with him the obsession of imitating and emulating antiquity, and this driving force implies an attempt to conquer time, to leave one's own contribution behind, one's mausoleum, hence at least an implicit desire for glory. Some literary figures were not very subtle about their design; Ronsard declaimed his own praise and that of his poems without shame or modesty. In Montaigne's case, the very act of writing about himself, of setting himself apart from others, of publishing himself his so-called self-portrait and confessions, already casts some shadows on any claim to modesty. Indeed, modesty belongs only to those who do not write.

Montaigne would like to parade in the guise of an ordinary human being, but he cannot convince, especially since he is writing the *Essays*—no common or easy task. And his consciousness that he is an average person and his saying so are already a tacit admission of vainglory: "I consider myself one of the common sort, except in that I consider myself so" (III : 17, 481); this declaration comes at the end of his life, after the bulk of his writing has been done, and makes his smile all the more apparent. One critic has even called this effort of wanting to give the impression of being ordinary "exorbitant and scandalous," yet very original.[16]

In fact, Montaigne eschews glory with his name only, not with his works. In his essay "Of Glory" (II : 16), he scorns the reputation that one's name may have because of its superficial impact and the lack of substance behind it: "We call it making our name great to spread and sow it in many mouths; we want it to be received there in good part, and to profit by this growth: that is the the most excusable element in this urge. But the excess of this malady goes so far that many seek to be talked about no matter how" (p. 474). What matters to Montaigne is not what others think of him but what he thinks of himself, and above all, whether he thinks that he is leading a good and useful life: "It is not for show that our soul must play its part, it is at home, within us, where no eyes penetrate but our own" (p. 472). On the other hand, he has written the essays to overcome "this colicky life" (II : 37, 575), the human condition, and to give therefore a meaning to his life. Furthermore, he would prefer to claim more readily paternity of the *Essays* than of human progeny, and this wish tells us much about a certain hierarchy of values and the place that his writings have in his life: "And I do not know whether I would not like much better to have produced one perfectly formed child by intercourse with the muses than by intercourse with my wife" (II : 9, 293). The writing of the *Essays* had become a duty for him, both a sedative and a goad to his conscience, the very purpose of his life. When an endeavor reaches such a central and all-encompassing function in one's life, becomes so consubstantial, it is hard to believe that posterity does not enter the picture, in spite of protestation to the contrary. After all, the *Essays* has a twofold purpose: to give Montaigne a spiritual balance and a self-mastery in order to be able to cope with life, and to communicate with others through time.

XI   *Disorder or Structure?*

This consciousness of posterity results not only from what Montaigne has to say, which remains valid for all at all times, but also from his commitment to creating a work of art, to leaving an aesthetic monument behind. However, in each essay form and content are inextricably intertwined, and any attempt to separate them occurs at the expense of the meaning of the text. Each essay is carefully orchestrated and structured in order to have an impact on the meaning. On the surface, disorder seems to reign, but the apparent ramblings of a mind operating through associations in a stream-of-consciousness process, always controlled, attest to the organic unity of the essay. In other words, whatever is mentioned, far from being disparate, always has a bearing on the central theme further to illuminate it, like the spokes of a wheel converging toward the hub. Then any stylistic excess aims either at pointing out the diversity and vacuity of thought and manner, or simply figures as a further excrescence to a point of view. The overwhelming dominant, however, is the omnipresence of a potent metaphoric language that fleshes out the thought; indeed, metaphors constitute an integral and inseparable part of thought, so that every allusion and example becomes an image to the point that everything is metaphor, and Montaigne thereby verges on the poet. He may continue to question knowledge, and reach some reconciliation with the impossibility of attaining it, but the doubt about the purpose and the function of the *Essays* diminishes considerably, even disappears, because with time, self-depreciation moves from a conviction to a game.

Upon reading any given essay, disorder appears to prevail, on the surface at least. An essay presents, from one vantage point, the meanderings of a mind—its promenades—operating through analogies and producing contradictions. It is generally open-ended; that is, it does not come to a clear logical conclusion according to the rules of classical perspective. Precisely, the concept of order/disorder should be a relativistic one; if cast against a fixed definition, it assumes an arbitrary definition, though still a valid one. On the other hand, the order or unity of a work can emerge from within it, and this kind of order is referred to as organic unity, i. e., a composite of connected elements, disparate on the surface, which constitute a whole. In this vein, a study of the second longest essay, "Of Vanity," demonstrates that a "variety of themes: vanity, the art of writing, the corruption of the times, estate management, flight from unpleasantness, travel, the diversity of custom, Roman history, the glories of Paris and Rome—to name but a few"[17] converge on the general topic suggested by the title of the essay and are all related to it. Organic unity also means that everything that a writer expresses, no matter how contradictory or disparate in nature, constitutes his personality, a totality acquired over a period of time.[18]

Although Montaigne defends his *modus operandi,* he still taunts the reader. A disparate composition simply reflects a disparate man and his world. What he does not say is that each essay does have at least a centrifugal structure, and what he implies is that his method may be superior to others which tend more to the one-dimensional:

I speak my meaning in disjointed parts, as something that cannot be said all at once and in a lump. Relatedness and conformity are not found in low and common minds such as ours. Wisdom is a solid and integral structure, each part of which holds its place and bears its mark. *Wisdom alone is wholly directed toward itself* [Cicero]. I leave it to artists, and I do not know if they will achieve it in a matter so complex, minute, and accidental, to arrange into bands this infinite diversity of aspects, to check our inconsistency and set it down in order. Not only do I find it hard to link our actions with one another, but each one separately I find hard to designate properly by some principal characteristic, so two-sided and motley do they seem in different lights. (III: 13, 824–25)

Furthermore, winking an eye, Montaigne claims to have strayed from the mainstream of his topic, and time and again with such phrases as "Now, to return to my subject" or "To return to our story" (I: 13, 152, 157) he pretends to regain a path he has actually never left. He plays a game with a reader who could quite easily believe him. Indeed, Montaigne does seem to diverge, to be disorganized in his thought and narrative patterns, but in fact these recalls have the exact opposite effect; they focus our attention on an order and an interconnection of themes. Even arguments bristling with self-esteem should not be taken too literally: "Fine materials are always in place, wherever you sow them. I, who have more concern for the weight and utility of the arguments than for their order and sequence, should not fear to place here, a little out of the way, a very beautiful story" (II: 27, 527–28). A metaphoric language based on the title of the essay gives further evidence that Montaigne toys with the notion of disorder: "Let us fall back to our coaches" (III: 7, 698); until finally he drops his mask and reveals that his back-to-order claim was nothing but a literary device: "Apropos or malapropos, no matter, they say in Italy . . ." (III: 11, 791).

If the structure within an essay is concentric, the structure among essays remains unexplored.[19] It is easy to see why certain essays are contiguous: "Of Pedantry" and "Of the Education of Children" (I: 25 and 26), "Of Moderation" and "Of Cannibals" (I: 30 and 31), "Of Three Good Women" and "Of the Most Outstanding Men" (II: 35 and 36). Yet one can assume that Montaigne had some pattern in mind when he arranged for publication the essays as we have them today. Is there, for example, a link from one essay to another throughout them? Such inner connections would certainly give the *Essays* a linear cohesion unknown at present. One ingenious critic has indulged in a numerical structural survey and noted that the number of essays in the second book is equal to two-thirds of the number in the first book, and the third book contains one-third as many essays as in the second book. Bearing in mind then the importance of the number 3 in the *Essays* (occurring also frequently in titles, for example) brings to the fore a challenging fact, but does it help to understand Montaigne?[20] Of more interest, along the same lines of numerical structure, is the essay that emerges at the dead center of all 107 essays: "Of Vain Subtleties" (I: 54). By its very position, this essay and its title cast a telling light on Montaigne's literary endeavor; they reveal the two faces of the epistemological coin: the limits and power of of knowledge.

In a way, the *Essays* is an arrangement of parallel stories and thoughts that never merge; this kind of structural evaluation gives the most credence to a linear construct of the essays and would provide one of the more fruitful avenues of investigation. The juxtaposition of points of view emulates Montaigne's model, Plutrarch's *Parallel Lives,* in which the binary division suggested by the title actually contains multifaceted fragments, or a sequence whose components are to be compared and contrasted.

XII *Verbal Accumulations and Verbal Play*

Montaigne's affinity for order and organic unity, in spite of his claims to the contrary, finds added support in his attitude toward and handling of words. Inordinate verbal outbursts, such as those that are Rabelais's trademark, do not frequently punctuate the *Essays*. If they did, they would exemplify an impulsive nature that abandons itself to the moment and to sentiments; on the contrary, Montaigne exhibits a calculated and deliberate temperament, controlled by a heavy dosage of irony. He does not trust words, is aware of their expressive inadequacy, but he has to use them. Long enumerations or asyndetons, although they occur somewhat rarely and for the most part in post-1588 additions, reflect this mistrust of words or a sense of plurality and diversity. Any presence of excessive verve, then, constitutes an excrescence in function of a basic tenet of the *Essays*, the multifariousness and difficulty of knowledge, and therefore is not a dangling adjunct to a composite whole.

In a passage reminiscent of Diogenes rolling his barrel in the prologue to Rabelais's *Third Book*, Montaigne unfurls a torrent of words to praise sign language with hands and head:

What of the hands? We beg, we promise, call, dismiss, threaten, pray, entreat, deny, refuse, question, admire, count, confess, repent, fear, blush, doubt, instruct, command, incite, encourage, swear, testify, accuse, condemn, absolve, insult, despise, defy, vex, flatter, applaud, bless, humiliate, mock, reconcile, commend, exalt, entertain, rejoice, complain, grieve, mope, despair, wonder, exclaim, are silent, and what not, with a variation and multiplication that vie with the tongue. With the head, we invite, send away, avow, disavow, give the lie, welcome, honor, venerate, disdain, demand, show out, cheer, lament, caress, scold, submit, brave, exhort, menace, assure, inquire. (II: 12, 322)

It may not be daring to remark irony in this passage, which showers words to stress their expressive limit and to favor a sign language. However, this use of asyndeton indicates a development toward a linguistic position; the verbal avalanche conveys a rhetorical import, since it aims at convincing the reader of an inverse stance;

hence the irony. The validity of this ironic stance is substantiated by a clear attack, made in an earlier essay, "Of the Vanity of Words" (I : 51), against rhetorical order and syntactical structure advocated by Cicero and his followers during the Renaissance.[21] Montaigne, then, opposes verbiage and verbose order, and he uses these techniques to scorn and confound those who adopt them and to defend the particular brand of structure and unity that the *Essays* propounds.

When less excessive verbal enumerations occur, on a more frequent basis than the longer accumulations of words, they illustrate the diversity and contradictions existing in human nature and in the universe, and therefore they become microcosms of the organic unity endemic to the *Essays*. The linear succession of words takes on a circular conceptual shape as they attempt to embrace and encompass the subjet. Precisely the more reasonable asyndetons constitute another means of essaying, of probing; they are verbal prisms reflecting a depth that can never be fully explored, since concentric circles continue to develop: "Bashful, insolent; chaste, lascivious; talkative, taciturn; tough, delicate; clever, stupid; surly, affable; lying, truthful; learned, ignorant; liberal, miserly, and prodigal: all this I see in myself to some extent according to how I turn; and whoever studies himself really attentively finds in himself, yes, even in his judgment, this gyration and discord" (II : 1, 242). The original version of this text offered only two adjectives. Time, the additions, provided more self-knowledge, more words, less ontological assurance, transformed the start of an ellipse into a circle, imparted a cohesion to the self. Words, then, are structure.

On a smaller scale Montaigne delights in juxtaposing two or three synonymous or antonymous words that clash through their meanings or sounds. The principal function of this stylistic trait is to underscore again the unity or cohesion of complementary, contradictory, or disparate elements. The high frequency of these techniques attests to their intimate integration with his thought and Weltanschauung:

d'une vifve et vehemente esperance . . . avec prudence et precaution . . .
plus pressant et plus poisant . . . on faict fructifier et foisonner le monde . . . .
(keen and vehement hope [III : 13, 856] . . . with prudence and precaution [I : 28, 140] . . . tighter and more oppressive [III : 9, 738] . . . they make the world fructify and teem with . . . [III : 13, 816])

Mais comment se laissent ils plier à la vraysemblance, s'ils ne cognoissent le vray? Comment cognoissent ils la sembance de ce de quoy ils ne cognoissent pas l'essence?

(But how can they let themselves be inclined toward the likeness of truth, if they know not the truth? How do they know the semblance of that whose essence they do not know? [II: 12, 422])

Je m'estudie plus qu'autre subject. C'est ma metaphysique, c'est ma physique.
(I study myself more than any other subject. That is my metaphysics, that is my physics. [III: 13, 821])

This play with etymologies, sounds, meanings reflects a serious grasp of the world: a unity of vision composed of disjointed elements. Although form and content fuse perfectly, a measure of a poet still emerges in the guise of a juggler with language who gives importance to the aesthetic quality of words. On occasion some of the sonorous word clashes may border on an excessive refinement, an affectation; yet at all times they implement meaning. Of course the comic or ironic effect sometimes produced can have an impact on the exact nature of the intended meaning. Thus the juxtaposition and play on words have a structural function; they exemplify Montaigne's belief that a fractured world, composed of several disconnected, related or unrelated, parts still forms a whole. They also have a bearing on meaning, on the possibility of knowledge, for these stylistic traits further reveal the cumulative and disparate nature of epistemology and ontology. Montaigne took great care in formulating these word clusters or clashes because he considered them an artful way to express himself in the *Essays*. Significantly enough, in a work of his that was not meant for publication, *Travel Journal to Italy,* but which saw the light almost two hundred years after its composition, these stylistic techniques occur much less frequently. [22]

XIII   *Syntax and Meaning*

If form and content are inseparable in Montaigne, as they should be in any good writer, it follows that the syntax of the *Essays* should also reflect their author's way of thinking. Indeed, sentence structure indicates Montaigne's manner of thinking, which in turn reflects his view of the world and of knowledge, because it features syntactical fragmentation, disconnection, suspension, ellipsis, antithesis. On the other hand, the syntax rather frequently follows a step-by-step pattern which has been called a "Senecan amble," that is, a succession of phrases or independent clauses resulting in a brisk pace but producing a slow tempo of the whole sentence and a composite concept.[23] In other words, for the most part the syntactical movement is rapid, but the emerging thought pattern is quite deliberate. It is no mere accident at all that one of the better passages illustrating Montaigne's syntax is the one in which he himself describes his own style:

> The speech I love is a simple, natural speech, the same on paper as in the mouth; a speech succulent and sinewy, brief and compressed, not so much dainty and well-combed as vehement and brusque: "The speech that strikes the mind will have most taste" [epitaph of Lucan]; rather difficult than boring, remote from affectation, irregular, disconnected and bold; each bit making a body in itself; not pedantic, not monkish, not lawyer-like, but rather soldierly, as Suetonius calls Julius Caesar's speech; and yet I do not quite see why he calls it so. (I: 26, 127)

The succession of phrases and independent clauses creating the Senecan amble and a semblance of disconnection through the lack of verbs are all here. One also finds the not atypical tail sentence, the last suspended clause, that puts into question what precedes it; this technique produces distantiation and uncovers the smile that evidences not only a game with the reader, but a refusal to a total commitment to a position, although it may still be there. Finally, this passage contains antithesis and the sonorous clashing of words that a translation cannot always render: *Non pedantesque, non fratesque, non pleideresque, mais plustost soldatesque* (not pedantic, not monkish, not lawyer-like, but rather soldierly); in this phrase, Montaigne forges new words to align a series of identical suffixes that convey a military rhythm not devoid of irony.

The apparent disconnection found in structure and syntax reflects naturally the impossibility of attaining knowledge, or its composite nature formed of variables and opposites. Yet a concise, so-called classical style can exercise the same function. Montaigne uses the straightforward maxim or proverb that expresses a distinct assertive notion in a paradoxical manner to undermine knowledge. The maxim or proverb occurs in the role of a refracting agency on which a developing argument converges and from which eventually a different if not opposite opinion emerges. The crystallizing

effect of the maxim is then destroyed by contrasting notions that
envelop it, and its presence buttresses only the argument of the
moment which is thereafter slowly undermined, but it can emerge
again as a constant after being tested. In discussing the durability
of a given government, Montaigne indicates that disorder and
confusion can keep it afloat because "All that totters does not fall"
(III: 9, 733). Yet a few lines below he notes that in his own time
identical conditions lead to political and societal disintegration:
"Now let us turn our eyes in all directions: everything is crumbling
about us in all the great states that we know, whether in Christendom
or elsewhere, take a look: you will find an evident threat of change
and ruin" (p. 734).

The maxim becomes a whetstone against which conflicting
ideas and observations are sharpened. Its moralizing and assertive
power acts in the same way as the title of an essay itself; a maxim
is the nucleus of an argument to be explored from several vantage
points, an extension of the title. Similarly in an earlier essay, "A
Custom of the Island of Cea," one finds that "The most voluntary
death is the fairest" (II: 3, 252). Is it natural death or suicide?
Voluntary as the only choice or under duress? Located toward
the beginning of the essay, this maxim, despite its clear assertion,
prefigures the thematic ambiguity that ensues. Of course a maxim
may encompass contradictions; in regard to the interrelationship
of political durability and confusion cited above, Montaigne
soon remarks that "Universal sickness is individual health" (p. 734);
one has to make the best of the existing situation, but the part
is more important than the whole. In fact, the proverbs and maxims
throughout an essay or the *Essays* constitute a sort of supra-
Senecan amble; they form a succession of independent clauses
that thematically clash with one another and refute thereby the
absolute or generalized knowledge expressed by each one of them.[24]

XIV *Knowledge Through Metaphor*

The abstract and diversified nature of thought and knowledge
makes Montaigne dependent on a predominant metaphoric
language that incarnates the gestations of his mind through a
vocabulary that leaves the daily rut of expression and thus succeeds
in freeing words from their usual connotational limits. Just as
Montaigne and the *Essays* are consubstantial, so are the creation

of images and his thought process and expression. If image and thought integrate perfectly, this fusion raises a puzzling critical question. Although the *Essays* conveys a sense of the limits and multifariousness of knowledge, the metaphoric language itself that delineates this condition does not suffer from any limitation or fragmentation. On the contrary, through its vividness and concreteness it seizes for the moment a thought pattern. It could be argued, then, that metaphors acquire an aesthetic value beyond their function of meaning that does not in any way, however, detract from their meaning. At least, the creation of an all-pervading metaphoric language conquers to an extent the inadequacy of words that Montaigne laments. And in the process there emerges Montaigne the poet, who gives ascendency to his imagination, despite its limits and dangers.

Metaphors render concrete and visual the abstract; this function explains their very high frequency, because through their vividness and palpability they remain superior to the limits, fluidity, and obscure nature of the knowledge they express. And to a degree, metaphors, by their very existence, overcome the limits of knowledge; they constitute the ultimate weapon against relative ignorance. No wonder, then, that some feel that everything is metaphor in the *Essays*.[25] Anything with only an apparent literal meaning can be transferred to another level: to Montaigne himself, to his act of writing the *Essays,* to the composite subject of the essay involved. And if there is transfer of meaning, there is metaphor. In and by themselves they become proof of, and a substitute for, discourse; they acquire thus an apodictic function.

It is generally agreed that comparisons are relatively rare and that metaphors increase in frequency in the later stages of the *Essays,* although this latter assertion is still open to interpretation. The paucity of comparisons has never been fully explained, yet it should not surprise. This form of metaphoric language does not allow for instantaneity between thought and expression, for the immediate consubstantiality between idea and language that is Montaigne's trademark. A comparison creates a detour that is not sufficiently integrated with the thought, artistically at least, and especially when confronted with the simultaneity of an image. In fact, the excess lies in the "like." In Montaigne's mind, the comparison must have smacked of artifice, despite its expressive, visual, and delineating potential: "It seems that the universe somehow suffers by our annihilation and that it has compassion for our state; because our vision, when altered, represents things to itself as being likewise altered, and we think they are failing it in proportion as it is failing them; like travelers at sea, for whom mountains, countryside, cities, heaven, and earth move right along with them and at the same pace . . ." (II: 13, 458).[26]

At first glance, metaphors do seem to be less frequent in the essays composed before 1580, that is, the bulk of the writing in the first two books. A more proper evaluation of this finding would be that, for the most part, the nature of the metaphoric language is different before 1580; it depends much more on the figurative meanings of tales and examples than it will later, and their high frequency in the first two books, higher than in the third, still produced therefore a thick and varied metaphoric base. An early essay, "Of the Uncertainty of Our Judgment" (I: 47), featuring the combat situations typical of the first two books, illustrates the multiple figurative meanings that can be attributed to examples and tales in it.

The essay presents four categories of cases which are argued pro and con, while the final solution is said to lie with fortune. The first one occurs in the context of vanity: Should one push on after being victorious, or be satisfied with a simple victory (cf. "Of Cannibals," I: 31)? The second rests on a background of avarice: Does a rich army, a well paid one, fight better than a poor one that has nothing to protect? The next set of examples deals with the question of wearing a mask: Should a military chief disguise himself or not to fight among and lead his soldiers? The final argument implies the notion of commitment and epistemology: does one remain in his own country or venture forth into foreign lands? In fact, this essay is concerned with the existential situation as it relates directly to the creative process, writing the *Essays*. Although apparently still not quite sure of himself, Montaigne has already made the decision to push on, keep on exploring and and writing, both to wear a mask and reveal his innermost self, to depend on the knowledge of others and his own experiences (the rich or poor army). In the last essays, with the advent and dominance of a more evident metaphoric language, the warring situations lose their inferred multiple figurative meanings and become an explicit image of self-serving dialectic checkmate and literary creation as in "Of the Art of Discussion": "What greater victory do you expect than to teach your enemy that he is no match for you? When you win the advantage for your proposition, it is truth that wins; when you win the advantage for order and method, it is you who win" (III: 8, 708).

Given the profusely and richly woven metaphoric fabric of the *Essays* and the perfect fusion between metaphor and thought, a systematization of images ought to bring out the focus of the content. And it does, but without any real surprises, precisely because of the intimate consubstantiality of image and thought. One system groups them in four categories, here in descending order of importance and frequency: movement and mutability [of the body, pure movement, elasticity, up and down inertia, torsion, stops and starts, water, walking, running, hunting and chasing, voyage], inside-outside [clothing, money, mask and face, interior-exterior, solid and coated, dyed], organic sensations [inner motivations, weight, thickness and fluidity, wind, sharpness, body as reflection of mind, sickness, food, receptacle and content, vegetal growth, taste, smells, music], visual images [eyes, plastic arts, light, fire, architecture].

These categories and their subdivisions still do not include all possible metaphoric denominations, but even if expanded further, they would all fall under the aegis of mobilism because of their intrinsic or contextual dynamism.[27] Such a finding remains most valid, since it integrates form and a fundamental aspect of the *Essays'* content. A typical metaphoric pattern of this kind pictures the "walkings" of the mind and the composite nature of its results, all cast in the usual somewhat ironic self-depreciation: "I have no marshal but fortune to arrange my bits. As my fantasies present themselves, I pile them up; now they come pressing in a crowd, now dragging in file. I want people to see my natural and ordinary pace, however off the track it is" (II: 10, 297). A most felicitous combination is achieved when a metaphoric movement created by the juxtaposition of images drawn from different realms meshes with a thinking and temporal mobilism to form a progressing entity: "Old age puts more wrinkles in our minds than on our faces; and we never, or rarely, see a soul that in growing old does not come to smell sour and musty. Man grows and dwindles in his entirety" *(L'homme marche entier vers son croist et vers son décroist)* (III: 2, 620).

According to the other synthesis, Montaigne's imagery deals essentially with the body.[28] Indeed, no one can object to this sort of conclusion, since the *Essays* is a self-portrait for which the

outside world exists in function of the self, and the total result
is the body of the essays: "It [mind] tells me that it is for my own
good that I have the stone; that buildings of my age must naturally
suffer some leakage. It is time for them to begin to grow loose
and give way" (III: 13, 836). Here the decaying "building" also
suggests a decaying mind (ironic) and society, and the essays
(ironic). Even if most images can be brought to bear on the body,
in a literal or figurative context, such a broad category, although
very useful, leans toward overgeneralization, cannot encompass
the whole metaphoric corpus, and therefore leaves some room
for dissatisfaction. However, further studies of the metaphoric
language itself will only produce a juggling and proliferation of
categories, which still bring further insights in the work. If the
study of the metaphoric language is to continue along fruitful
lines, it should stress the multiple dimensions of the image without
tying it to a synthesizing formula. The presence of the word-image
is self-evident, its prismatic quality not always so. To limit is to be
anti-Montaigne in spirit.

Less obvious than the word-image is what could be called the
metaphoric tableau in the guise of a tale, for example, that illustrates a moral point but then assumes a totally different meaning
along unexpected lines, different, at least, from those stated. When
the transferred meaning does appear, then the literal plane becomes
dynamic, and words that at first were frozen in their usual connotation come to life in a different realm. In "Of Repentance"
(III: 2), Montaigne laments that often the pleasure derived from
repentance makes vice excusable, if not the very vehicle for sin:
"On others (in whose regiment I belong) vice weighs heavily, but
they counterbalance it with pleasure or some other consideration,
and endure it and lend themselves to it for a certain price; viciously,
however, and basely. Yet it might be possible to imagine a disproportion so extreme that the pleasure might justly excuse sin,
as we say utility does; not only if the pleasure was incidental and
not a part of the sin, as in theft, but if it was in the very exercise
of the sin" (p. 616).

Then, with no other explicit connection than "as in theft" follows
a rather lengthy recollection-tale that depicts a version of a Renaissance Robin Hood:

The other day when I was at Armagnac, on the estate of a kinsman
of mine, I saw a country fellow whom everyone nicknames the Thief. He
gave this account of his life: that born a beggar, and finding that by earning

his bread by the toil of his hands he would never protect himself enough against want, he had decided to become a thief; and he had spent all his youth at this trade in security, by virtue of his bodily strength. For he reaped his harvest and vintage from other people's lands, but so far away and in such great loads that it was inconceivable that one man could have carried off so much on his shoulders in one night. And he was careful besides to equalize and spread out the damage he did, so that the loss was less insupportable for each individual. He is now, in his old age, rich for a man in his station, thanks to this traffic, which he openly confesses. And to make his peace with God for his acquisitions, he says that he spends his days compensating, by good deeds, the successors of the people he robbed; and that if he does not finish this task (for he cannot do it all at once), he will charge his heirs with it, according to the knowledge, which he alone has, of the amount of wrong he did to each. Judging by this description, whether it is true or false, this man regards theft as a dishonorable action and hates it, but hates it less than poverty; he indeed repents of it in itself, but in so far as it was thus counter-balanced and compensated, he does not repent of it. This is not that habit that incorporates us with vice and brings even our understanding into conformity with it; nor is it that impetuous wind that comes in gusts to confuse and blind our soul, and hurls us for the moment headlong, judgment and all, into the power of vice. (III: 2, 616)

On the literal level, this story illustrates a "counterbalanced and compensated" vice that does not elicit repentance and substantiates therefore the framing thesis. On a figurative plane, however, the Thief is Montaigne, the writer of the *Essays* who has cannibalized other writers and thinkers in order to avoid "poverty" of mind and lack of quality of life, and finds himself now "rich for a man in his station, thanks to this traffic," and obviously not repentant for it. He deplores his heavy dependence on others ("he reaped his harvest and vintage from other people's lands, but so far away and in such great loads"), though he drew from a variety of sources to protect himself and his sources ("he was careful besides to equalize and spread out the damage he did"). The *Essays* is an unfinished product, in appearance at least, and he will confess to posterity which will have to judge whether he did wrong, whether the undertaking was worthwhile—"if he does finish this task (for he cannot do it all at once), he will charge his heirs with it, according to the knowledge, which he alone has, of the amount of wrong he did to each."

In fact, this tale has all the trappings of an autobiographical allegory in the light of his creative life; no wonder, then, if it stands out as one of the longer exemplary stories found in the *Essays*. By its relative inordinate length, Montaigne draws careful attention to this story, to himself the writer, to the validity of his labor. In the final analysis, both literally and more often metaphorically, the *Essays* is reduced to Montaigne the writer looking at himself writing, questioning his enterprise, and in the process becoming more assured than ever of the writing's integral participation to his serenity and spiritual liberty, thus of its indispensability.

XV   *The Voyage*

This integration of the creator and his creation explains the microcosmic function of the subject and the metaphor of the voyage. Every time the word "voyage" occurs, one can substitute for it Montaigne's *modus operandi,* the purpose of the *Essays,* or the act of writing. In essence, then, *voyage,* either as substantive or verb, conveys the same multiple meanings that *essay* has. On a more obvious plane, the physical or literal voyage has an anthropological and educational goal; Montaigne travels to Italy in order to expose himself to different customs and gain a better perspective on his own. On the figurative level, and in this same vein, the voyage is equivalent to his readings. Both literally and metaphorically, traveling is a form of communication, an opportunity for change and exchange, and for learning from one another not facts but psychological and moral motivations: "For this reason, mixing [*commerce*] with men is wonderfully useful, and visiting foreign countries, not merely to bring back, in the manner of our French noblemen, knowledge of the measurements of the Santa Rotonda, or . . . how much longer or wider Nero's face is in some old ruin there than on some similar medallion, but to bring back knowledge of the characters and ways of those nations, and to rub and polish our brains by contact with those of others" (I: 26, 112).[29] Significantly enough, this discussion of travel occurs in "Of the Education of Children"; the *Essays,* too, educates and is the result of a "commerce," an exchange process between sources and experiences.

Traveling is the very yeast that leads to further writing. It fertilizes the mind and provides Montaigne with new observations and a rekindled sense of relativism that find their way into the *Essays;* indeed, the subject itself of the voyage comes more vividly and explicitly to the fore in the third book (cf. "Of Vanity," III: 9), composed after his sojourn in Italy. But the object sought through travel, through writing the essays, is not something better, but rather something different that can be rubbed against what one already knows or has experienced: "I ordinarily reply to those who ask the reason for my travels, that I know well what I am fleeing from, but not what I am looking for" (III: 9, 743). The voyage keeps the mind working through the discovery of new settings, of new encounters, both topographically and epistemologically, not to mention the self-knowledge adduced. Travel-writing is a medicine against restlessness and the human condition and an escape from the obligations and tedium of daily life, household and financial responsibilities being in fact the least disturbing. The cause of this anguish provides at the same time its very remedy; diversity leads to irresolution, which in turn produces the only measure of satisfying and possible wisdom; although each essay constitutes an entity within itself, it remains unfinished and suspended, and inevitably leads to another and yet another. Yet any of them suffices in itself: "I know well that if you take it literally, this pleasure in traveling is a testimony of restlessness and irresolution. And indeed these are our ruling and predominant qualities. Yes, I confess, I see nothing, even in a dream or a wish, that I could hold myself to; variety alone satisfies me, and the enjoyment of diversity, at least if anything satisfies me. In traveling, I am encouraged by the very fact that I can stop without loss, and that I have a place where I can turn aside from it comfortably" (III: 9, 756).

Ultimately, and to a large extent, Montaigne travels for the sheer pleasure of traveling. The voyage—the thinking, the self-discovery, the self-awareness, the writing—is an end in itself. Yet he prefers certain modes of travel to others. He does not care for coach, litter, or boat; however, if, on occasion, boat it has to be, then he had rather have somewhat rough waters than calm ones. His favorite means of transportation is horseback (III: 6, 687). Figuratively then he rejects modes of travel which he cannot himself control (coach, litter, boat), but in which he must rely on others to carry him, unless a testing situation is involved (rough waters); on horseback he can be his own master and set himself off from others or rise above others. To travel is to change locale, to change positions, and to remain available to do so, but the voyage must not be harsh or brusque; Montaigne seeks what he calls a moderate agitation, an evenness of pace—the substantial and formal description of the *Essays*.

Traveling affords a measure of freedom; in fact, it allows a welcome uprooting from conventional time and space. It does not have actually to take place; the mere knowledge that such possibilities exist already satisfies. When the human journey fails, the imaginary one begins:

I am so sick for freedom, that if anyone should forbid me access to some corner of the Indies, I should live distinctly less comfortably. And as long as I find earth or air open elsewhere, I shall not lurk in any place where I have to hide. Lord, how ill could I endure the condition in which I see so many people, nailed down to one section of this kingdom deprived of the right to enter the principal town and the courts and to use the public roads, for having quarreled with our laws! (III: 13, 821)

The constraints of the human condition, of society, of the political situation change but still remain. If Montaigne himself for the moment feels free, he has no assurance of continuance in the free state. To gain this assurance of freedom, liberty of spirit, he chooses the literary voyage, the writing of the *Essays,* that conquers, so far as is possible, the human contingencies.

The perfect knowledge that Montaigne has progressively acquired is the conviction of the worthwhileness of a journey dealing with imperfections. He has not altered anything in the epistemological world, but he has delineated an ontological universe. He has not drawn straight lines, but he has traced configurations. He embraced much, knowing that totally he would grasp little. Yet he assimilated all he dealt with. He grappled with the one-dimensional tools of knowledge—words—and forged multidimensional prismatic verbal mirrors that look at each other, become each other's equivalent, and in which he looks at himself, the writer facing the problems of the craft of fiction. His main task is to communicate, as he looks at himself trying to communicate. And he succeeded, witness the *Essays*—the felicitous result of a so-called failure.

CHAPTER 5

Conclusion

T HE most objective, and perhaps the simplest, conclusion
to Montaigne would be to cite or discuss the last pages or
lines of his *Essays;* but this ending does not represent his last
thoughts. As a matter of fact, we do not know what his last writings
are; they could be found just as well among the last additions to
one of the first essays as among those to one of the last essays, or
somewhere in the middle. For Montaigne there is no beginning,
middle, or end; his universe is not a linear one, not even a circular
one, but a kaleidoscopic one; or better still a cubist one, because
he returns to the first level of his written thought, juxtaposes and
superposes other opinions that give a question a multidimensional
depth of a temporal and spatial nature. Yet to offer no conclusion,
because of this working process, would be a most simplistic conclusion.

Since Montaigne appears to defy synthesis, one can evince this
knotty situation by offering an open-ended conclusion in temporal
terms, that is, Montaigne's impact on posterity. Just to cite a
few examples of this impact, one begins with Pierre Charron's
On Wisdom, published at the end of the sixteenth century, that
heavily plagiarizes the *Essays.* In the next century Pascal scorns
Montaigne, whom he must really admire, though he does not
agree with him. In the eighteenth century Montaigne's critical
judgment appeals to Bayle, who is also trying to harness and
control a morass of knowledge and to decide whether the Moderns
are superior to the Ancients. Later in that century, Diderot's sardonic
yet vastly probing mind is attracted to his Renaissance peer. The
post-Romantic era sees the beginning of some of the best criticism
on Montaigne by Sainte-Beuve, some of which still has not been
surpassed. During that same time, the author of the *Essays* finds
staunch admirers in Emerson and Pater. In our own times, Gide
bent the *Essays* to suit his own needs and substantiated some
of his own obsessions in Montaigne's availability and flexible
morality. On the other hand, a confrontation with Proust brings
out affinities in the peripatetic and prismatic treatment of time and

space, while Camus and Sartre share with Montaigne some similar
attitudes toward death and the existential meaning of life. Still
to be explored would be a comparison between Montaigne and
Wittgenstein in the inherent limits on the power of language to
communicate. [1]

It is precisely Montaigne who appeals to the modern sensitivity
because he cannot be presented to the reader in a compactly-
wrapped cellophane package. His many facets remain juxtaposed
and cannot be interfused. The very title of each essay is like a
Mallarmean symbol that encompasses a kinetic multimeaning.
There will never be an overwhelming consensus on his religion,
his political and social views, or even on the question of the evolution of his thought, and fortunately so because this disagreement
attests to Montaigne's vitality. However, of Montaigne's modernity
there is absolutely no doubt. Nescience and the difficulty of communication, for example, occupy a fundamental role in the *Essays*.
The search for an evanescent self, or the quest for a permanent
identity, provides another pervading element. Then Montaigne
asks himself: What is the substance of life? What gives life a meaning? And he sinuously threads his way between mind and body.
He grapples incessantly with the questions of choice, commitment,
involvement; these recurrent themes are at the same time the
nightmare and the purpose of his life.

Ultimately Montaigne faces the human condition with hope—
still tinted with some apprehension. If he is able to tranform the
inescapable into an acceptable and happy situation, he can also
see the dark side of what everyone else considers happiness or a
positive situation. He does not differentiate as much between good
and evil, wrong and right, as between consciousness and unconsciousness; he advocates keeping the physical and mental eye
open and an awareness of what one is doing. To these questions
and dilemmas Montaigne found the answer by writing the *Essays,*
an enterprise few can emulate. His privileged status is transformed
into our learning experience; Montaigne the individualistic Everyman becomes the I we each one of us seek within ourselves. Montaigne the cultist of Art assumes, then, the proportions of a Magus
who succeeds in communicating through mystification.

Notes and References

Chapter One

1. See E. V. Telle, "A propos du mot *essai* chez Montaigne," *Bibliothèque d'Humanisme et Renaissance,* 30 (1968), 225–47; A. Blinkenberg, "Quel sens Montaigne a-t-il voulu donner au mot *Essais* dans le titre de son œuvre?" *Bulletin de la Société des Amis de Montaigne,* 29 (Jan.–March, 1964), 22–32; R. A. Sayce, *The Essays of Montaigne: A Critical Exploration* (Evanston, Ill.: Northwestern Univ. Press, 1972), pp. 20–22; Alan M. Boase, "The Early History of the *Essai* Title in France and Britain," in *Studies in French Literature Presented to H. W. Lawton* (Manchester: Manchester Univ. Press, 1968), pp. 67–73.

2. All English citations of Montaigne refer to Donald M. Frame's translation of the *Essays* in *The Complete Works of Montaigne* (Stanford, Calif.: Stanford Univ. Press, 1957). The Roman numerals refer to the book, the first Arabic number to the chapter in that book, and the second Arabic number to the page. The same pagination is also applicable to the paperback edition of this translation (Stanford University Press, 1965).

3. Cf. J. Starobinski, "Distance et plénitude," *Mercure de France,* 348 (July, 1963), 402.

4. It is surprising that one of the better Montaigne scholars of the first half of the century, Fortunat Strowski, believes that the last book, Book III, which he falsely claims was written in a year, shows notable weaknesses of composition and style vis-à-vis the first two books, mostly because the last book was too rapidly put together, cf. *Montaigne* (Paris: Alcan, 1931), p. 38. Actually the very opposite is true and so accepted; the last essays are the most masterly and comprehensive ones.

Chapter Two

1. Two vols., (Paris: Hachette, 1908); rev. ed., 1933, and reprint (New York: Burt Franklin, 1968).

2. Donald M. Frame, *Montaigne's Discovery of Man: The Humanization of a Humanist* (New York: Columbia Univ. Press, 1955), p. 48.

3. Henri Peyre, *Literature and Sincerity* (New Haven: Yale Univ. Press, 1963), pp. 36–37.

4. Cf. Alexandre Micha, *Le Singulier Montaigne* (Paris: Nizet, 1964), pp. 12, 21. Cf. also "For all the variability and change, by temperament and by judgment Montaigne was fundamentally static rather than kinetic . . . . He sought harmony within, not conflict" (Frame, p. 52).

5. Among the many sources for these prevalent views on evolution, see the whole second volume of Villey's work; Floyd Gray, *Le Style de Montaigne* (Paris: Nizet, 1958), pp. 189–92; Jean-Yves Pouilloux, *Lire les Essais de Montaigne* (Paris: Masper, 1969), pp. 94–98.

6. Cf. Imbrie Buffum, "The Basic Baroque Categories as Exemplified by Montaigne," *Studies in the Baroque from Montaigne to Rotrou* (New Haven: Yale Univ. Press, 1957), pp. 12—13.

7. Cf. Pouilloux, pp. 101–2.

8. Barbara C. Bowen, *The Age of Bluff: Paradoxical Ambiguity in Rabelais and Montaigne* (Urbana: Univ. of Illinois Press, 1972), p. 138.

9. Although this position is held by most present leading critics, see esp. Hugo Friedrich, *Montaigne*, trans. Robert Rovini (Paris: Gallimard, 1968), pp. 30–32.

10. For a further discussion of ambiguity see Pouilloux, pp. 28–32; Micha, pp. 217–19; Bowen, pp. 103–27.

11. R. A. Sayce, "Baroque Elements in Montaigne," *French Studies,* 8 (1954), 15. On the use of antithesis in Montaigne, see Friedrich, pp. 387–88; Buffum, pp. 42–43; Michaël Baraz, *L'Etre et la connaissance selon Montaigne* (Paris: Corti, 1968), pp. 134–38; Frank P. Bowman, *Montaigne: Essays* (London: Arnold, 1965), pp. 30–32.

12. Cf. Rosalie L. Colie, *Paradoxica Epidemica: The Renaissance Tradition of Paradox* (Princeton: Princeton Univ. Press, 1966).

13. See Alfred Glauser, *Montaigne paradoxal* (Paris: Nizet, 1972), pp. 85–87. Yves Delègue, "Du paradoxe chez Montaigne," *Cahiers de l'Association Internationale des Etudes Françaises,* 14 (1962), 241–53.

14. To consider the paradoxes in Montaigne in a negative light is, we think, erroneous; cf. Fortunat Strowski, *Montaigne* (Paris: Alcan, 1931), p. 153.

15. One of the better treatments of Bergsonian mobilism in Montaigne can be found in Albert Thibaudet, *Montaigne*, ed. Floyd Gray (Paris: Gallimard, 1963), pp. 163–88; cf. also Gérard Genette, "Montaigne bergsonien," in *Figures* (Paris, 1966), pp. 139–43.

16. Cf. Micha, p. 107.

17. Villey, I, 6; II, 535, 546.

18. Michel Butor, *Essais sur les Essais* (Paris: Gallimard, 1968), p. 161.

19. Cf. Françoise Joukovsky, *Montaigne et le problème du temps* (Paris: Nizet, 1972), pp. 215–37; this study argues most convincingly for the continuity of thought and crisis found in the additions in relation to the first version of an essay. See also Bowen, *The Age of Bluff*, p. 138; here the author asserts that in "Of Liars" (I: 9), for example, there is essentially no difference among the three versions of the essay, just a shift of emphasis, and the original version contains "by implication everything that is in the final version."

20. R. A. Sayce, "Montaigne's Style," *The Essays of Montaigne: A Critical Exploration*, pp. 280–312.

21. Cf. Glauser, *Montaigne paradoxal*, p. 45.

22. Cf. Joukovsky, pp. 241–45.

23. Jean Starobinski, "Montaigne en mouvement," *Nouvelle Revue Française*, 85 (February, 1960), 265.

Chapter Three

1. Cf. for example, the lengthy description of Seneca's death, with an emphasis on its psychological implications, in the essay "Of Three Good Women" (II: 35).

2. Friedrich, p. 78. Even a more traditional critic like Strowski concedes that stoicism for Montaigne is only a means, not an end, not a doctrine nor a firm belief (p. 118).

3. Villey, I, 209.

4. Thibaudet, *Montaigne*, pp. 285–86; cf. Gray, *Le Style de Montaigne*, p. 196.

5. Cf. Philip Hallie, *The Scar of Montaigne* (Middletown, Conn.: Wesleyan Univ. Press, 1966), p. 23.

6. For general studies on skepticism, see Richard H. Popkin, *The History of Skepticism from Erasmus to Descartes* (Assen, Netherlands: Van Gorham, 1960); Philip Hallie, *Skepticism, Man and God* (Middletown, Conn.: Wesleyan Univ. Press, 1964); D. C. Allen, *Doubt's Boundless Sea* (Baltimore: Johns Hopkins Press, 1966). Cf. also Donald Frame, "Skepticism: Temper and Tool," in *Montaigne's Essais: A Study* (Englewood Cliffs, N. J.: Prentice-Hall, 1969), pp. 22–31.

7. For a discussion of the concept of nature in the *Essays*, see Villey, II, 375–436; Frame, *Montaigne's Discovery of Man*, pp. 100–108; Micha, pp. 122–33; Baraz, pp. 32–33; Neal Dow, *The Concept of Man and Term "Nature" in Montaigne's Essays* (Philadelphia: Univ. of Pennsylvania Press, 1940).

8. One reason, for example, that Montaigne admires Plutarch so much is that "of all the authors I know, [he] is the one who best combined art with nature and judgment with knowledge" (III, 6, 685).

9. This passage is a post-1588 addition and brings to the fore again Montaigne's admiration for Socrates' behavior facing death with an uncommon courage. This admiration for the Greek philosopher's "natural" conduct before death receives its most elaborate development in the third book, especially in the essay "Of Physiognomy" (12, 805–7).

10. One of the better comprehensive discussions of death can be found in Friedrich, pp. 270–315.

11. Thibaudet, 569.

12. The translation here is my own. A list of all the sentences inscribed on the beams of Montaigne's library can be found in the *Oeuvres complètes*, ed. M. Rat and A. Thibaudet (Paris: Bibliothèque de la Pléiade, 1965), pp. 1419–25. This particular one is no. 23, p. 1422.

13. Cf. Frieda S. Brown, *Religious and Political Conservatism in the Essais of Montaigne* (Geneva: Droz, 1963).

14. C.-A. Sainte-Beuve, *Port-Royal*, II (Paris: Hachette, 1867), 406–9; 412–21; 425–31; 441–42. For a very cogent criticism of the Sainte-Beuve position see Donald M. Frame, "Did Montaigne Betray Sebond?" *Romanic Review*, 38 (1947), 297–329.

15. Villey, II, 326, 329.

16. Maturin Dréano, *La Religion de Montaigne* (Paris: Nizet, 1969), pp. 183–93; the first version of this study appeared in 1936. A similar approach to a Montaigne *bon catholique* can be seen in another book also written by a man of the Church, Armand Müller, *Montaigne* (Paris: Desclée du Brouwer, 1965), in the series Les Ecrivains devant Dieu. A good synthezing view of Montaigne's religion was given by Frame, "Religion," in *Montaigne's Essais: A Study*, pp. 65–71. The ambivalence of Montaigne's religion has been very well shown by R. A. Sayce, "Montaigne and Religion," in *Essays of Montaigne*, pp. 202–32.

17. For a discussion of the concept of imagination see I. D. McFarlane, "Montaigne and the Concept of the Imagination," in *The French Renaissance and Its Heritage: Essays Presented to Alan M. Boase* (London: Methuen, 1968), pp. 117–38; Charles Sécheresse, "Montaigne et l'imagination," *Bulletin de la Société des Amis de Montaigne*, 27 (1963), 18–29; Frederick Rider, "Of the Power of the Imagination," in *The Dialectic of Selfhood in Montaigne* (Stanford, Calif.: Stanford Univ. Press, 1973), pp. 5–23.

18. Strowski, p. 214.

19. Micha, pp. 172–75.

20. Friedrich, p. 121.

21. Baraz, pp. 104–9.

22. This distinction between the man and his work is very well made by Sayce, *Essays of Montaigne*, pp. 231–32.

23. A basic study of the subject of the human condition in the *Essays* is still Erich Auerbach's "L'Humaine condition," in *Mimesis*, trans. Willard Trask (Garden City, N. Y.: Doubleday Anchor Books, 1957), pp. 249–73.

24. Hallie, *Scar of Montaigne*, p. 152.

25. Cf. Jean Starobinski, "Montaigne et la relation à autruy," *Saggi e Ricerche di Letteratura Francese*, 9 (1968), 83–91; Rider, "The Need for Self-Distance," pp. 5–23.

26. For Montaigne the nobleman and its impact on the *Essays*, see Jean-Pierre Boon, *Montaigne gentilhomme et essayiste* (Paris: Editions universitaires, 1971).

27. It may be worth recalling that Rabelais in the prologue to his *Third Book* takes a similar stance. Comparing himself to Diogenes rolling his barrel [i.e., Rabelais writing his book], he implied that such action is as valid if not superior to the activities of the Corinthians who are building fortifications.

28. Further discussions of the concept of commitment can be read in Friedrich, pp. 260–65; Baraz, pp. 34–46; Hallie, pp. 118–32, 146–50; Frame, *A Biography*, pp. 223–45; Frieda Brown, "'De la solitude'; A Re-examination of Montaigne's retreat from Public Life," in *From Marot to Montaigne* (Lexington, Ky.: Univ. of Kentucky Press, 1972), pp. 137–46.

29. Cf. Joukovsky, pp. 144–68.

30. See Walter Kaiser, "Rabelais's Panurge," in *Praisers of Folly* (London: Gollancz, 1964), pp. 101–92; Verdun-Louis Saulnier, *Le Dessein de Rabelais* (Paris: Société d'édition d'enseignement supérieur, 1957).

31. The most recent and comprehensive study of the concept of education in the *Essays* and of Montaigne's education itself can be found in Roger Trinquet, *La Jeunesse de Montaigne* (Paris: Nizet, 1972), pp. 161–560. The author places this concept, first in a pro- and then a contra-Erasmian framework, that is, from the theoretical to the practical plane, and centers it further about a pro and con attitude toward the utility of spoken Latin; Montaigne had been taught to speak Latin before he learned French. See also Paul Porteau, *Montaigne et la vie pédagogique de son temps* (Paris: Droz, 1935); and Frame, *A Biography*, pp. 39–45.

32. Gray, *Style*, pp. 211–24.

33. For a discussion of the mask and its relation to the inner and outer being see Starobinski, "Montaigne et la relation à autruy," 79–82; and the recent very enlightening chapters by Hélène-Hedy Ehrlich, "Le dedans et le dehors," "Le masque et le jeu," and "Le monde et le théâtre: réalité et forme," in *Montaigne: la critique et le language* (Paris: Klincksieck, 1973), pp. 38–44, 56–69, 109–24.

34. Several months after I had written these remarks on the "theatricality" of education, similar ones appeared in Rider, pp. 78–80.

35. "Bond" or "tie" actually does not quite translate Montaigne's metaphor *couture*, which means seam or suture and expresses the union of two disparate entities into a perfectly fused whole.

36. Cf. Frame, *Discovery of Man*, pp. 21–29; Strowski, p. 91; Friedrich, pp. 256–58.

37. Cf. Anthony Wilden, "Montaigne's *Essais* in the Context of Communication," *Modern Language Notes*, 85 (1970), 454–78.

Chapter Four

1. Montaigne uses the word *inscience* for lack of knowledge or the impossibility of knowing. To convey the positive connotations of this

word, as opposed to ignorance, one would have to coin a word such as "disknowledge" or "unknowledge." Our own "nescience" in English does not quite have the same connotation as *inscience.*

2. "Thus in this matter of knowing oneself, the fact that everyone is seen to be so cocksure and self-satisfied, that everyone thinks he understands enough about himself, signifies that everyone understands nothing about it . . . " (III: 13, 823).

3. The best study on Montaigne with respect to the concept of knowledge and lack of it is by Michaël Baraz, *L'Etre et la connaissance,* although no critic can study Montaigne without alluding to this fundamental stance in the *Essays.* See also Baraz' article "Sur la notion d'inscience chez Montainge," *De Ronsard à Breton* (Paris: Nizet, 1967), pp. 42–50, which is a reduced version of what appears in the book (pp. 89–117). Cf. Arnaldo Pizzorusso, "Sul 'metodo' di Montaigne: le occasioni del giudizio," *Da Montaigne a Baudelaire: prospettive e commenti* (Roma: Bulzoni, 1971), pp. 21–38.

4. This is a reference to Ecclesiastes 1:2, "Vanity of vanities, all is vanity." The first part of this translation is my own, because the one by Professor Frame does not express the ellipsis intended by Montaigne.

5. The question of Montaigne's attitude toward language has begun to receive critical attention rather recently and still deserves further inquiry; cf. Friedrich, pp. 95–99, 169–71; Hallie, pp. 73–97; Glauser, pp. 11–13; Richard Regosin, "Language and the Dialectic of the Self in Montaigne's *Essais,*" in *From Marot to Montaigne* (Lexington: Univ. of Kentucky Press, 1972), pp. 167–75. Yvonne B. Rollins, "Montaigne et le langage," *Romanic Review,* 64 (1973), 258–72. The most elaborate and penetrating study to date is by Hélène-Hedy Ehrlich, *Montaigne: la critique et le langage,* pp. 70–108. For a general treatment of the inadequacy of words see Michel Foucault, *Les Mots et les choses* (Paris: Gallimard, 1968).

6. Pouilloux, p. 114.

7. The best arguments along this line, followed by others who take the same stance, are made very convincingly by Herbert Lüthy, "Montaigne, or the Art of Being Truthful," *Encounter,* 2 (November 1953), 33–44.

8. For the advocates of irony see among others Micha, pp. 104–5, 190; Friedrich, p. 28; Gray, *Style,* pp. 28–29; Bowen, p. 115; Strowski, pp. 320, 328. The difficulty of being sincere in self-portraiture has been pointed out by Peyre, *Literature and Sincerity,* pp. 42–43, and Lionel Trilling alludes obliquely to Montaigne's questionable sincerity by quoting Rousseau's judgment: *Je mets Montaigne à la tête des faux sincères qui veulent tromper en disant vrai.* in *Sincerity and Authenticity* (Cambridge: Harvard Univ. Press, 1972), p. 59.

9. Edgar Wind, *Pagan Mysteries in the Renaissance* (New York: Norton, 1968), p. 236.

10. Cf. Zoe Samaras, *The Comic Element of Montaigne's Style* (Paris:

Nizet, 1970), pp. 116, 147–48; Donald Frame's discussion of the "Happy paradox" in *Montaigne's Discovery of Man*, pp. 85–88, as well as his "A Detail in Montaigne's Thought: The Source of Our Ignorance Is the Source of Our Happiness," *Word*, 5 (1949), 159–65; Kieth C. Cameron, *Montaigne et l'humour* (Paris: Les Lettres Modernes, 1966); André Berthiaume, "Montaigne humoriste," *Etudes Littéraires,* 4 (1971), 187–207.

11. For the topic of self-depreciation in Montaigne, see Marie-José Southworth, "Les Remarques dépréciatives de Montaigne au sujet de son livre," *Bulletin de la Société des Amis de Montaigne*, 27 (Oct.–Dec., 1971), 19–26; Cf. also Bowen, pp. 121–25; Frame, *Montaigne's Discovery*, pp. 84–85; Glauser, pp. 49, 66, 72.

12. This concept of the aesthetics of negligence has been treated by John C. Lapp, "Montaigne and Some Lines from Virgil," in *The Aesthetics of Negligence: La Fontaine's Contes* (Cambridge: The Univ. Press, 1971), pp. 14–30.

13. Cf. Friedrich, p. 350.

14. Although every booklength study on Montaigne almost has to take into account the question of memory, see in particular S. John Holyoake, "Montaigne's Attitude Toward Memory," *French Studies* 25 (1971), 257–70.

15. At present one excellent book exists on the question of time in the *Essays*—by Françoise Joukovsky, *Montaigne et le problème du temps*; Georges Poulet's chapter on time in Montaigne remains also most valuable, in *Studies in Human Time*, trans. Elliot Coleman (Baltimore: Johns Hopkins Univ. Press, 1956), pp. 39–49; and another recent study on the subject, while stressing the concept of the present, does not clearly delineate the problem; see Ricardo Quinones, "Montaigne," in *The Renaissance Discovery of Time* (Cambridge: Harvard Univ. Press, 1972), pp. 204–42. Cf. also Henry Hornik, "Time and Periodization in French Renaissance Literature: Rabelais and Montaigne," *Studi Francesi*, 39 (Sept.–Dec., 1969), 477–81.

16. Starobinski, "Montaigne et la relation à autruy," p. 101.

17. Buffum, "The Basic Baroque Categories as Exemplified by Montaigne," p. 76; cf. pp. 60–76.

18. Cf. Floyd Gray, "The Unity of Montaigne in the '*Essais*'", *Modern Language Quarterly*, 12 (1961), 79–86; R. A. Sayce, "The Unity of the Essays," in *The Essays of Montaigne*, pp. 327–34; Michaël Baraz, "Le Sentiment de l'unité cosmique chez Montaigne," *Cahiers de l'Association Internationale des Etudes Françaises*, 14 (1962), 211–24. The same concept of organic or cosmic unity in Montaigne has been the subject of a penetrating recent book by Olivier Naudeau, *La Pensée de Montaigne et la composition des Essais* (Geneva: Droz, 1973).

19. Studies on the structure of individual essays have been made by

Baraz, "Sur la structure d'un essai de Montaigne (III, 13: 'De l'Expérience')," *Bibliothèque d'Humanisme et Renaissance*, 23 (1966), 265–81; W. G. Moore, "Montaigne's Notion of Experience," in *The French Mind: Studies in Honour of Gustave Rudler* (Oxford: Clarendon Press, 1952), pp. 34–52; René Etiemble, "Sens et structure dans un essai de Montaigne ['Des coches,' III: 6]," *Cahiers de l'Association Internationale des Etudes Françaises*, 14 (1962), 263–74; Robert Griffin, "Title, Structure and Theme of Montaigne's 'Des coches,'" *Modern Language Notes*, 82 (1967), 285–90.

20. Cf. Butor, pp. 71–79, 173–74.

21. Cf. Robert D. Cottrel, "Le Style anticicéronien dans l'oeuvre de Montaigne et de Sponde," *Romanic Review*, 59 (1958), 16–29.

22. Cf. R. A. Sayce, "The Style of Montaigne: Word-Pairs and Word-Groups," in *Literary Style: A Symposium*, ed. Seymour Chatman (New York: Oxford Univ. Press), p. 405; a somewhat different version of this study, stressing less the word cluster aspect, can now be found in the author's recent book, *The Essays of Montaigne*, pp. 280–312. For other studies on word clusters in the *Essays*, see Samaras, "Clashing Words and Play on Words," pp. 116–48; Gray, *Style*, pp. 109–23; Friedrich, pp. 386–90. The structural aspect of this technique which we attempt to develop is not stressed by these critics.

23. Cf. Morris W. Croll, "The Anti-Ciceronian Movement: 'Attic' and Baroque Prose Style," in *Style, Rhetoric, and Rhythm*, eds. J. Max Patrick et al. (Princeton: Princeton Univ. Press, 1966), pp. 3–233; in this section see especially the following essays: "Juste Lipse et le mouvement anticicéronien à la fin du XVIe et au début du XVIIe siècle," "Attic Prose: Lipsius, Montaigne, Bacon," and "The Baroque Style in Prose." Cf. also George Williamson, *The Senecan Amble: A Study of Prose from Bacon to Collier* (Chicago: Univ. of Chicago Press, 1951), pp. 121–49. See, as well, Samaras, "Sentence Forms," pp. 61–115; Gray, *Style*, pp. 23–30, 70–95.

24. Up to now proverbs and maxims in the *Essays* have been studied in relation to Montaigne's thought and not so much stylistically or structurally to substantiate that thought. Cf. Edmond Lablénie, *Montaigne: auteur de maximes* (Paris: Société d'édition d'enseignement supérieur, 1968); Louis Hippeau, "Montaigne et La Rochefoucauld," *Bulletin de la Sociétè des Amis de Montaigne*, 11 (1967), 41–50; Sister M. Katherine Elaine, "The Moral Force of Montaigne's Proverbs," *Proverbium*, 3 (1965), 33–45; Roy E. Leake Jr., "Montaigne's Gascon Proverb Again," *Neophilologus*, 52 (1968), 248–55; there is one exception that deals with the comic element in the maxims, in Samaras, pp. 107–15.

25. Beginning with Sainte-Beuve, *Port-Royal*, II, 443 (Book III, Ch. 3).

26. For studies of comparisons see Gray, "La Comparaison," in *Style*, pp. 137–50; Yves Delègue, "Les Comparaisons dans les *Essais* de Mon-

taigne," *Revue d'Histoire Littéraire de la France*, 66 (1966), 593–613.

27. Cf. Thibaudet, "Les Images de Montaigne," pp. 505–66; and Gray, "Les Images et la pensée de Montaigne," *Style*, pp. 151–81.

28. Cf. Baraz, "Images et vision de l'être," pp. 47–86; for an earlier version of this chapter see "Les images dans les *Essais* de Montaigne," *Bibliothèque d'Humanisme et Renaissance*, 27 (1965), 361–94. For other studies on imagery see Walter Schnabel, *Montaignes Stilkunst, eine Untersuchung vornehmlich auf Grund seiner Metaphern* (Breslau and Oppeln: Priebatsch, 1930); Gilbert Mayer, "Les Images dans Montaigne d'après le chapitre de l'Institution des enfants," *Mélanges de philologie et d'histoire littéraire offerts à Edmond Huguet* (Paris: Boivin, 1940), pp. 110–18; Frame, *Montaigne's Essais*, pp. 93–96; Samaras, "Metaphor and Comparison," pp. 47–60.

29. For the relationship between Montaigne's travels and the *Essays*, see Imbrie Buffum, *L'Influence du voyage de Montaigne sur les Essais* (Princeton: n.p., 1946); Craig B. Brush, "The Essayist is Learned: Montaigne's *Journal de voyage* and the *Essais*," *Romantic Review*, 62 (1971), 16–27; cf. Albert Thibaudet, "Le Style de voyage," *Nouvelle Revue Française*, 29 (1927), 377–85.

Chapter Five

1. Cf. Grace Norton, *The Influence of Montaigne* (New York and Boston: Houghton, Mifflin, 1908); Alan M. Boase, *The Fortunes of Montaigne: A History of the Essays in France, 1580–1669* (London: Methuen, 1935); Donald M. Frame, *Montaigne in France 1812–1852* (New York: Columbia Univ. Press, 1940); Charles Dédeyan, *Montaigne chez ses amis anglo-saxons* (Paris: Boivin, 1946); Maturin Dréano, *La Renommée de Montaigne en France au XVIIIe siècle* (Angers: Editions de l'Ouest, 1952); Craig B. Brush, *Montaigne and Bayle: Variations on the Theme of Skepticism* (The Hague: Nijhoff, 1966); Jerome Schwartz, *Diderot and Montaigne: The Essais and the Shaping of Diderot's Humanism* (Geneva: Droz, 1966); Frieda S. Brown, "Peace and Conflict: A New Look at Montaigne and Gide," *French Studies*, 25 (1971), 1–9.

Selected Bibliography

PRIMARY SOURCES

1. Important Editions of Montaigne's Works

Les Essais. Nouvelle édition, augmentée de quelques lettres de l'auteur, par Pierre Coste. 3. vols. London-Paris, 1724. After the 1595 edition by Mlle de Gournay, the standard edition into the nineteenth cèntury.

Essais. Texte original de 1580, avec les variantes des éditions de 1582 et 1587. ed. R. Dezeimeris and H. Barckhausen. 2 vols. Bordeaux: 1870–73. A standard edition until the more modern ones appeared. The strata of variants for the first two books are still most useful.

Essais, ed. Fortunat Strowski *et al.* 5 vols. Bordeaux: Pech, 1906–33. Called the "Edition Municipale." First edition to take into account the additions of the Bordeaux Copy instead of depending solely on the Gournay edition.

Essais, ed. Fortunat Strowski. Paris: Hachette, 1912. The photographic reproduction of the Bordeaux Copy showing Montaigne's handwritten additions of 1588–92.

Oeuvres complètes, ed. Dr. Armand Armaingaud. 12 vols. Paris: Conard, 1924–41. In Addition to critical studies by the editor, this edition includes the *Travel Journal, Letters,* the *Natural Theology* of Raymond Sebond, works by La Boétie. The classic critical edition.

Essais, ed. Pierre Villey. 3 vols. Paris: Alcan, 1930–31. A standard critical edition that gives strata indications and dates of composition.

Essais, ed. Jean Plattard. 6 vols. Paris: Roches, 1931–33. Reprinted by the Société Les Belles Lettres in 1946–48. Also a fine standard critical edition and somewhat more readily available.

Essais, ed. Maurice Rat. 2 vols. Paris: Garnier, 1962. A useful and frequently-used classroom edition.

Oeuvres complètes, ed., A. Thibaudet and M. Rat. Paris: Bibliothèque de la Pléiade, 1962; repr. 1965 and 1972. Now the standard edition of the complete works; unfortunately the Italian parts of the *Travel Journal* appear only in the French translation.

Essais, ed. Pierre Michel. 3 vols. Paris: Le Livre de Poche, 1966. A practical edition in modernized French.

L'Italia alla fine del secolo XVI. Giornale del Viaggio di Michele de Montaigne in Italia nel 1580 e 1581, ed. Alessandro D'Ancona. Città di Castello: Lapi, 1889; rev. ed. 1895. The matrix edition for all subsequent editions of the *Travel Journal*; also contains a most valuable bibliography of French travelers to Italy.

Journal de voyage, ed. Louis Lautrey. Paris: Hachette, 1906; rev. ed. 1909. Still the standard critical edition, reproduces much of D'Ancona.

Journal de voyage, ed. Charles Dédeyan. Paris: Société Les Belles Lettres, 1946. Useful for its relative availability and for the integrity of the Italian parts that are translated into French on a facing page.

2. Translations

The Essayes, trans. John Florio. London: V. Sims for E. Blount, 1603. The first English translation, now also available in recent editions; valuable above all for its linguistic flavor, which matches closely that of the French text.

The Essays, trans. Charles Cotton. 3 vols. London: T. Basset, M. Gilliflower, and W. Hensman, 1685–86. A standard for the next two centuries.

The Works. Essays, trans. by Charles Cotton, rev. by the younger William Hazlitt; *Diary of a Journey* and *Letters* trans. by the younger William Hazlitt. London: Templeman, 1842. This same edition, but containing more letters, was later published in New York: Edwin C. Hill, 1910.

The Essays, trans. George B. Ives; intr. Grace Norton. 4 vols. Cambridge: Harvard Univ. Press, 1925. Valuable because it gives strata indications, although the text is expurgated.

The Essays, trans. Jacob Zeitlin. 3 vols. New York: Knopf, 1934–36. Until recently the standard American translation, still important for its critical apparatus.

The Complete Works, trans. Donald M. Frame. Stanford, Calif.: Stanford Univ. Press. 1957. Contains the *Essays, Travel Journal,* and *Letters.* The current standard edition.

The Complete Essays, trans. Donald M. Frame. Stanford: Stanford Univ. Press, 1965. Paperback edition of above translation of the essays, same pagination.

Essays and Selected Writings, ed. Donald M. Frame. New York: St. Martin's Press, 1963. Noteworthy and useful for its bilingual presentation.

Selected Essays of Montaigne in the Translation of John Florio, ed. Walter Kaiser. Boston: Houghton Mifflin, 1964. A useful selection to taste the flavor of the first English translation.

The Journal of Montaigne's Travels. Trans. W. G. Waters. 3 vols. London: John Murray, 1903.

The Diary of Montaigne's Journey to Italy in 1580 and 1581. trans. E. J. Trechmann. London: Hogarth Press, 1929.

Giornale del Viaggio di Michel de Montaigne in Italia, ed. Glauco Natoli. 3 vols. Florence: Parenti, 1959. Italian translation of the *Travel Journal* noteworthy for its introduction and the sixteenth-century maps of the cities Montaigne visited.

Saggi, trans. and ed. Fausta Garavini. 2 vols. Milan: Adelphi, 1966; reprint Milan: Mondadori, 1970, in paperback. Current standard Italian translation valuable for its critical apparatus and introductions.

3. Specialized Bibliographies

CABEEN DAVID C., ed. *A Critical Bibliography of French Literature. The Sixteenth Century.* Syracuse: Syracuse Univ. Press, 1956, nn. 1488–1806.

CIORANESCU, ALEXANDRE. *Bibliographie de la littérature française au 16e siècle.* Paris: Klincksieck, 1959, nn. 15277–16007.

FRAME, DONALD M., "What next in Montaigne Studies?" *French Review*, 36 (1963), 577–87. Reviews past scholarship and looks to the future.

FRESCAROLI, ANTONIO. "Gli studi montaignani in questi ultimi cinquant' anni," *Aevum*, 33 (July–Aug., 1959), 416–35. A look at Montaigne scholarship for the first half of this century.

MICHEL, PIERRE. "Bibliographie montaigniste pratique (1580–1950)," *Bulletin de la Société des Amis de Montaigne*, 1 (1957), 62–80.

————. "Direction de travail sur Montaigne pour les Agrégatifs," *Bulletin de la Société des Amis de Montaigne*, 5 (1973), 43–109. A most useful bibliographical, historical, and thematic article to study Montaigne.

PLATTARD, JEAN. *État présent des études sur Montaigne.* Paris: Belles Lettres, 1936. More useful for suggested studies rather than for complete list of studies already done.

TANNENBAUM, SAMUEL A. *Michel de Montaigne: A Concise Bibliography.* New York: Samuel A. Tannenbaum, 1942. Rather exhaustive but not critical.

SECONDARY SOURCES

1. Periodicals and Commemorative Publications

Bulletin de la Société des Amis de Montaigne (1913 to present but with the interruptions: 1915–20, 1922–36). Vastly improved in these last years, contains some very serious articles. Published four times a year.

Cahiers de l'Association Internationale des Etudes Françaises (1962).

Mémorial du Ier Congrès International des Études Montaignistes (Bordeaux-Sarlat, ler-4 Juin 1963). Bordeaux: Taffard, 1964.

L'Esprit Créateur 8 (1968).

Europe (Jan.–Feb., 1972).

2. Important Critical Studies

AUERBACH, ERICH. "L'Humaine Condition," *Mimesis*, trans. Willard Trask. Princeton: Princeton Univ. Press, 1953, pp. 285–311; reprint in Doubleday Anchor Books, Garden City, N.Y.: Doubleday, 1957, pp. 249–73. Goes much beyond the beginning of "Of Repentance" (III: 2), which he analyzes admirably.

BARAZ, MICHAËL. *L'Être et la connaissance selon Montaigne.* Paris: Corti, 1968. One of the best books published in the last few years.

BATTISTA, ANNA MARIA. *Alle origini del pensiero politico libertino: Montaigne e Charron,* Milan: Giuffrè, 1966. Especially useful for the relationship between Machiavelli and Montaigne.

BOASE, ALAN M. *The Fortunes of Montaigne: A History of the Essays in France, 1580–1669.* London: Methuen, 1935. A thorough study of the period.

BOON, JEAN-PIERRE. *Montaigne gentilhomme et essayiste.* Paris: Editions Universitaires, 1971. Studies the relationship between the nobleman and the essayist.

BOWEN, BARBARA C. *The Age of Bluff: Paradox and Ambiguity in Rabelais and Montaigne.* Urbana: Univ. of Illinois Press, 1972. An illuminating and accurate study on Montaigne.

BOWMAN, FRANK P. *Montaigne: Essays.* London: Arnold, 1965. A concise, crisp, and valuable introductory study.

BROWN, FRIEDA S. *Religious and Political Conservatism in the Essais of Montaigne.* Geneva: Droz, 1963. An able study of still thorny topics.

BRUSH, CRAIG B. "The Essayist is Learned: Montaigne's *Journal de voyage* and the *Essais,*" *Romanic Review,* 62 (1971), 16–27. Notes the absence of learning, images, and *gauloiseries* in the *Journal* as opposed to their presence in the *Essays.*

BUFFUM, IMBRIE. *L'Influence du voyage de Montaigne sur les Essais.* Princeton: Princeton Univ. Press, 1946. Stresses the importance of Montaigne's travel on the organic unity of the *Essays.*

———. *Studies in the Baroque from Montaigne to Rotrou.* New Haven: Yale Univ. Press, 1957. Very valuable for the study of style and its relation to ideas.

BUTOR, MICHEL. *Essais sur les Essais.* Paris: Gallimard, 1968. At times a very provocative book.

CAMERON, KEITH C. *Montaigne et l'humour.* Paris: Les Lettres Modernes, 1966. A short, able, but not exhaustive treatment of the subject.

CHATEAU, JEAN. *Montaigne psychologue et pédagogue.* Paris: Vrin, 1964. Latest book on subject still along traditional lines.

CROLL, MORRIS W. "The Anti-Ciceronian Movement: 'Attic' and Baroque Prose Style," *Style, Rhetoric, and Rhythm,* ed. J. Max Patrick *et al.* Princeton: Princeton Univ. Press, 1966, pp. 1–233. Important for the concept of the Senecan amble in Montaigne's syntax and style.

DÉDEYAN, CHARLES. *Essai sur le Journal de Voyage de Montaigne.* Paris: Boivin, 1946. Attempts to show how the travels to Italy formed Montaigne's personality and judgment, not always successful.

DRÉANO, MATURIN. *La Religion de Montaigne.* Paris: Beauchesne, 1936; rev. ed. Paris: Nizet, 1969. Montaigne the firm Catholic shown here is not always convincing.

EHRLICH, HÉLÈNE-HEDY. *Montaigne: la critique et le langage.* Paris: Klincksieck, 1972. Innovative and stimulating, focuses on a structuralist approach.

EMERSON, RALPH WALDO. "Montaigne: or, the Skeptic," *Representative Men.* Boston: Houghton Mifflin, 1903, pp. 147–86. Reveals the affinities between the two men.

FRAME, DONALD M. *Montaigne's Discovery of Man: The Humanization of a Humanist.* New York: Columbia Univ. Press, 1955. A masterful book on the development of Montaigne's thought.

———. *Montaigne: A Biography.* New York: Harcourt, Brace, 1965. The standard English work on the subject.

———. *Montaigne's Essais: A Study.* Englewood Cliffs, N.J.: Prentice-Hall, 1969. A useful introduction to Montaigne.

FRIEDRICH, HUGO. *Montaigne,* trans. Robert Rovini. Paris: Gallimard, 1968. One of the best books on Montaigne.

GIDE, ANDRÉ. "Presenting Montaigne," *The Living Thoughts of Montaigne,* trans. Dorothy Bussy. New York: Longmans, Green, 1939, pp. 1–27. The making of a Gidean Montaigne.

GLAUSER, ALFRED. *Montaigne paradoxal.* Paris: Nizet, 1972. A most perceptive study of the thematic complexities of the *Essays.*

GRAY, FLOYD. *Le Style de Montaigne.* Paris: Nizet, 1958. Still the best book on the subject.

———. "The Unity of Montaigne in the *Essais,*" *Modern Language Quarterly,* 22 (1961), 79–86. Good study on the organic unity of the *Essays.*

HALLIE, PHILIP P. *The Scar of Montaigne: An Essay in Personal Philosophy.* Middletown, Conn.: Wesleyan Univ. Press, 1966. Contains some very level-headed and penetrating discussions.

ILSLEY, MARJORIE H. *A Daughter of the Renaissance: Marie le Jars de Gournay.* The Hague: Nijhoff, 1963. Most informative on Montaigne's adoptive daughter.

JOUKOVSKY, FRANÇOISE. *Montaigne et le problème du temps.* Paris: Nizet, 1972. A commendable contribution to the subject; not easy, but rewarding reading.

KELLERMAN, FREDERICK, "Montaigne's Socrates," *Romanic Review,* 45 (1954) 170–77. Details Montaigne's emulation of the Greek philosopher's wisdom.

LA CHARITÉ, RAYMOND. *The Concept of Judgment in Montaigne.* The Hague: Nijhoff, 1968. A good synthesizing work showing the diversity of meanings of judgment.

LANSON, GUSTAVE. *Les Essais de Montaigne: étude et analyse.* Paris: Mellottée, 1930; reprint 1948. A sensitive general study injected with much common sense.

LAPP, JOHN C. "Montaigne and some lines from Virgil," *The Esthetics of*

Negligence: La Fontaine's Contes. London and New York: Cambridge Univ. Press, 1971. Illuminating on Montaigne's self-depreciation, and his style.

MARCU, EVA. *Répertoire des idées de Montaigne*. Geneva: Droz, 1965. A very useful working tool; cites and organizes texts according to thematic topics.

MICHA, ALEXANDRE. *Le Singulier Montaigne*. Paris: Nizet, 1964. Contains sensible critical evaluations; strikes down the traditional evolution theory.

MICHEL, PIERRE. *Montaigne*. Bordeaux: Ducros, 1970. A useful introductory study, quite good for Montaigne's fortune in France and abroad.

MÜLLER, ARMAND. *Montaigne*. Paris: Desclée De Brouwer, "Les Ecrivains devant Dieu," 1965. Presents a fairly well catholicized Montaigne.

NAUDEAU, OLIVIER. *La Pensée de Montaigne et la composition des Essais*. Geneva: Droz, 1972. Challenging for attempt to differentiate between what Montaigne says and what he means.

NORTON, GRACE. *Studies in Montaigne*. New York: MacMillan, 1904. More valuable for broad discussions on style than for specific essays analyzed.

PAPIC, MARKO. *L'Expression et la place du sujet dans les Essais*. Paris: Presses Universitaires de France, 1970. A syntactical study of the location of the subject, does not show sufficiently the relation between syntax and content.

PORTEAU, PAUL. *Montaigne et la vie pédagogique de son temps*. Paris: Droz, 1935. A standard work on the topic of education, though a bit dated now.

POUILLOUX, JEAN-YVES. *Lire les Essais de Montaigne*. Paris: Masper, 1969. Stresses a nonsynthesized Montaigne.

POULET, GEORGES. "Montaigne," *Studies in Human Time*, trans. Elliot Coleman. Baltimore: Johns Hopkins Press, 1956, pp. 39–49. Very penetrating pages.

RIDER, FREDERICK. *The Dialect of Selfhood in Montaigne*. Stanford: Stanford Univ. Press, 1973. Some very refreshing views on old topics.

SAINTE-BEUVE, CHARLES-AUGUSTIN. *Port Royal*. 7 vols. Paris: Hachette, 1867–71, Vol. II, 379–453. Still contains some of the best pages on Montaigne's style.

––––––. "Montaigne en voyage," *Nouveaux lundis*. 14 vols. Paris: Lévy, 1870–83, Vol. II, 156–77. Good pages on Montaigne's need to travel.

SAMARAS, ZOE. *The Comic Element of Montaigne's Style*. Paris: Nizet, 1970. A thorough stylistic dissection of the *Essays*, bringing forth a convincing comic strain.

SAYCE, RICHARD A. "Montaigne et la peinture du passage," *Saggi e Ricerche di Letteratura Francese*, 4 (1963), 9–59. Stresses the theory of mobilism.

––––––. *The Essays of Montaigne: A Critical Exploration*. Evanston:

Northwestern Univ. Press, 1973. One of the best and most sensible books on Montaigne.

SOLMI, SERGIO. "La salute di Montaigne," *Cultura,* 12 (1933), 281–99; reprinted in *La salute di Montaigne e altri scritti di letteratura francese* (Milan and Naples: Ricciardi, 1952), pp. 3–32. Now also found as one of the introductions to the Garavini translation. Stresses consubstantiality and healthfully facing the human condition; still one of the better general articles on Montaigne.

STAROBINSKI, JEAN. "Montaigne et 'la relation à autruy'," *Saggi e Ricerche di Letteratura Francese,* 9 (1968), 77–106.

———. "Distance et plénitude," *Mercure de France,* 348 (1963), 400–409. Two splendid but difficult articles dealing with self-realization.

STROWSKI, FORTUNAT. *Montaigne.* Paris: Alcan, 1931, 2nd ed. A standard work which also espouses the evolution theory.

THIBAUDET, ALBERT. *Montaigne,* ed. Floyd Gray. Paris: Gallimard, 1963. Emphasizes mobilism, also most valuable for its parts on style and imagery.

TRINQUET, ROGER. *La Jeunesse de Montaigne.* Paris: Nizet, 1972. For a long time to come, the definitive work on the first twenty-five years of Montaigne's life.

VILLEY, PIERRE. *Les Sources et l'évolution des Essais de Montaigne.* 2 vols. Paris: Hachette, 1933, 2nd ed.; reprint New York: Burt Franklin, 1968. Although the evolution theory has been repeatedly challenged, this work remains fundamental for the sources and the dating of the *Essays*

YATES, FRANCES A. *John Florio: the Life of an Italian in Shakespeare's England.* Cambridge: Cambridge Univ. Press, 1934. The standard study on Montaigne's first English translator, who happened to be Italian.

Index